THE NEW MILLIONAIRE

Biblical Secrets To Making Millions And Keeping It!

Revised Edition

Apostle Steve Lyston

Library of Congress Control Number: 2018906605
ISBN: 978-1-7320-7621-1
(Previously published under ISBN 978-1-4251-8414-8 by Trafford
Publishing)

Original Edition of this book is available from Library and Archives
Canada at www.collectionscanada.ca/amicus/index-e.html

Edited by: Hazeth B. Williams, Marsha A. Williams-McCormack,
Michelle R. Lyston
Cover Design by: Johann D. A. Williams
Layout: Nicole Bertram

This book is designed to provide accurate and authoritative
information with regard to the subject matter covered. This
information is given with the understanding that the author is not
engaged in rendering legal, professional advice. Since the details of
your situation are fact-dependent, you should seek the services of a
competent professional.

Published in the United States of America

DEDICATION

This book is dedicated, first, to the *Holy Spirit of God*, without Whom I could not have carried out this task of honor.

Secondly, I dedicate this book to

My wife, Pastor Dr. Michelle Lyston

My children - Shevado Lyston, Hannah Lyston and Joshua Lyston

And to the memory of our son, *Moses Lyston* who went back to be with the Lord
(Joshua 1: 1 – 5)

Thirdly, to all the New Millionaires, close family and friends who stuck with us through the fire – God bless you abundantly.

Finally, this book is dedicated to the men and women of God who struggle through difficult times and seasons. God has not forgotten you – He is about to take you into your wealthy places!

A SPECIAL THANK YOU

To every person who has supported and stood with us over the years. I appreciate each and every one of you and all that you do for the Lord. Continue to trust, stand and believe in God! Your labor of love is not in vain.

TESTIMONY

After authoring the book End Time Finance: God's Guide For You, Your Business, Your Church and Your Nation, I thought all would be well. But God decided to take us on another journey. He began teaching me about what a New Millionaire should be.

God, through the power of His Holy Spirit carried us through the fire. We realized that in order to get wealth the right way – even the wealth of knowledge, wisdom and understanding, it would take much pain and suffering.

We realized that the world was designed to take your wealth and keep you in bondage/debt, which is the number one (1) health hazard. It is difficult to find an honest business person. They will all be nice to you, and convince you to purchase or engage in business transactions with them. However, after that, you are left in debt with high interest rates.

Everyone wants to be a millionaire, but no one wants to abide by the principles of God. While business persons expect to get grace and compassion from God, they don't extend it to their customers and clients. For them it's all about the money and making it at any cost. That is why there is so much bankruptcy in our world today. God is repaying all for the practices they have embraced and executed.

We have been through great suffering, pain and injustice – some we can't even make mention of at this point. We couldn't even afford health insurance at all. But God has kept us!

We have learnt through our suffering, to trust God only, put Him first at all times, love our family, abide by His principles, have faith, Tithe, and Sow, Sow, Sow! Giving, and giving to the right cause, is the only action that will take us elevate us to the place of promise.

We know now, more than ever, that while we may see the mega-church leaders and television preachers giving eloquent speeches regarding prosperity and giving, they themselves have ignored the opportunities God has given them to practice what they preach! I implore all, always ask the Lord to show you where the fertile soil is in which you must sow your seed. Don't look at the size, personality or outward appearance of the ministry, church or leaders when making the decision to sow. Study Mark 4.

On many occasions we asked for help under the instruction of the Lord. They ignored our cries for help. The Lord allowed us to go through this, so that we don't make the same mistakes. He wanted us to see the state of Christendom and learn from their mistakes.

Ensure that you never underestimate, undermine or ignore the local church. Help the man and/or woman of God and pour into their lives by sowing and praying for them. They may not tell you all the details of what they are going through; but you need to ask the Lord, *'In what way can I be of help to the man and/or woman of God and to Your house?'*

Remember, all the wealth belongs to God. Both God and Satan are calling the nations to declare their loyalty! Where do you stand? God has already won, will you settle for second best?

We will never forget that in the midst of typing this book, we lost our house and our son, Moses, in the same period. This was one of the most difficult and painful periods we had ever had. But *nothing* will separate us from the love of our God, and in our weakness, His strength is made manifest.

The entire experience also taught us something valuable. Many will say that they will stand with you, but when adversity strikes, they fall away.

God allowed us to go through all this so that He could use this book – this tool – to let you know that, regardless of the stage or state you are in – even if you are a bankrupt, former millionaire, you can still make it, through God!

God is transferring the wealth of the wicked now (including some of His own who have abused God's favor and wasted His resources) and is transferring it to the just. The focus – whether of the Church, Government or Private Sector – must never be on infrastructure only, but on developing human resources. Each person is born with a vision and a purpose. Sometimes all they need is a helping hand. Many are in shelters, homes and on the streets. Sadly we spend more money on pets, drugs and junk than we do on reaching out to someone or helping someone to fulfill their purpose. We even spend more money on research when all the information we need can be gathered by simply going out there and connecting with someone and helping them. The New Millionaire is one who recognizes that and is prepared to go the extra mile to do it.

TABLE OF CONTENTS

Chapters   ***Pages***

Foreword
Preface
Introduction

Chapter 1: Making A New Move   19

Chapter 2: Basic Biblical Economics   26

Chapter 3: Debt   46

Chapter 4: About Money And Financial
            Matters   70

Chapter 5: Money Must Do Good Things   83

Chapter 6: Needed … Bankers With
            Compassion   86

Chapter 7: Business   95

Chapter 8: Money Management In
            Business   107

Chapter 9: The Book Of Luke   116

Chapter 10: The Holy Spirit In Business
            And Nations   123

FOREWORD

A wise businessman knows that he cannot trust those around him with the inner workings of his operations and secret strategies until they have 'declared their hand' and their loyalty to him – not until they have made their commitment to him completely. This is a **God-principle**. He is the original Businessman, and so, if we desire to reap the benefits of His blessings in any area of our lives so that we can become a New Millionaire, it can only truly come when we first make a genuine commitment and declare our loyalty to Him!

This book reveals how the Word of God can be applied to business and to the affairs of nations. It explains to the average man, the business executive and the governmental officials their varying responsibilities to God, the Kingdom of God, the House of God and the people of God that serve in His house.

There are many businessmen, nation leaders and leaders at every other level who, while they seek to bring solutions to make themselves, their organizations, and even the nation more successful, fail to bring about lasting success; and lose their families and wealth in the process.

The Church worldwide is now feeling the pangs of famine, and many church leaders have turned to other jobs to supplement their basic existence. This in turn, divides their attention and diminishes their effectiveness in the ministry, ultimately pulling them away from their calling. As a result, the rest of the world feels the effects of the 'part-time church'.

This book also clearly shows how applying the principles of God to every aspect of our existence, and investing in the Kingdom of God can not only bring great successes, numerous victories and unity within the family, and even to a national level; but will also bring us into closer and right relationship with God – the True and Living God!

The season has changed and the wealth and resources are shifting! The transference of wealth to the faithful in the Body of Christ is about to manifest, and in order to receive and maintain it, we must all abide by Biblical Principles. We must be ready to acquire the true wealth God desires to release!

The battle is on! Let the transfer begin!

Pastor Michelle Lyston
Restoration World Outreach Ministries Inc

PREFACE

This book was written for non-believers and believers in Jesus Christ, to open their eyes to the truth. It was also written as a guide for individuals, businesses and nations who desire to have the real solutions to the issues they face by the employment of Biblical Principles to daily transactions and as a result become the New Millionaire.

While the world is plunging into darkness, particularly in Trade, Commerce and Morality, it is not, nor can it ever be again, business as usual!

Many economists, financial strategists and politicians have been attempting to come up with various solutions for the problems affecting the nations, but to no avail. The fact of the matter is that all must realize that God is in charge of your finance and the national economies. He is the one who gives the power to get wealth – Deuteronomy 8: 18

This book will teach you to come out of debt using Biblical Principles, and also how to get increase and breakthrough, particularly during famine/recession. It deals with the purpose of the Holy Spirit in Business, and in the lives of individuals and nations. It was also written to help you understand how to turn your mistakes into your platform for wealth.

In addition to this, this book helps you to uncover and expose un-Godly practices of creditors and lenders.

As you read this book, it will edify you and strengthen your foundation to help to make you *The New Millionaire!*

INTRODUCTION

The New Millionaire is a book inspired by the greatest CEO that ever lived – Jesus Christ – in order to teach you how to tap into the things of God to get wealth and maintain it as well. Many people are going through great economic and financial problems; many companies are merging and some are filing for bankruptcy! There are serious financial situations and famine facing us now!

We have seen and continue to see many clubs and fellowships being formed, and they are charging thousands for memberships to teach you to be a millionaire, but we need to ask a question- *'Does it help?'* The answer is *'NO!'* Those who were once making millions are no longer making it, so they say *'Let us put a course package together – a **How-To-Get-Rich** program – give it a catchy name'* all in an effort to make up the shortfall they incurred in regular business! They put these programs together under the guise of trying to help you acquire wealth based on their success and the knowledge they have acquired about what is happening in the market!

What is happening is that God is always the major shareholder in every organization, but He has been neglected by man in business.

The major shareholder is now evaluating and giving you your appraisal score what is your score? If you are below satisfaction you are in trouble.

As a businessman/businesswoman in these End-Times you must look into the following:

➤ What role does God play in your organization

➤ Take a good long look at the methods you use to get your wealth

➤ Do you pay Tithes and Sow Seed

➤ Am I helping the poor and using my resources and clout in the business community to help others

➤ To be a New Millionaire one must learn about Biblical Principles, you can't be wealthy and maintain it without taking instructions for the source that releases blessings.

Trying to understand a market that is not really controlled by earthly forces is crazy. God is in control of the world markets not man, and He does not depend on the state of the market to bless you! God is not influenced by any earthly limitations. He controls Times and Seasons – He changes times and seasons!

God wants you to get knowledge from Him first, according to Matthew 6: 33; then He will grant you the desires of your heart.

Spending $6000 to learn man-made principles and practically nothing else will not help you invest in the kingdom and receive wisdom to get and maintain wealth. Only Biblical Principles will help you to achieve and maintain such success!

In light of all this, welcome to your first step toward becoming a *New Millionaire!*

Chapter 1

MAKING A NEW MOVE

The world has entered into an era of uncertainty on two levels – globally and locally – particularly in the area of economic development. A paradigm shift has taken place, which will ultimately affect individuals, nations and businesses and how they operate – and that includes your business or nation.

In the past few years, you have seen several natural disasters affect various nations – hurricanes in North America and the Caribbean; earthquakes, floods, typhoons, a Tsunami in Asia – all of which have had and continue to have serious negative effects on the world's economy and especially on our own local businesses – large and small. International currency instability continues, crime continues to increase in addition to countless issues.

There is therefore the need for you and your organization to re-focus in an effort to remain or become more successful.

You now need the Apostles and Prophets who have a governmental anointing, the gifts of Nehemiah who re-built the economic stability of a nation; and also the anointing of Joseph and Daniel who offered solutions to the kings. They have the prophetic insight to see what lies ahead and what is necessary to deal with the problems that will arise.

Biblical Economics

Simply put, *'Biblical Economics'* is *'the employment of economic strategies and guidelines garnered through divine revelation of the written Word.'* It deals with every aspect of business, including Marketing, Finance and Investment, Human Resources and Training, Production, Sales, Staff Morale and even Security.

As a result, you and your organization will become the beneficiaries of growth; increase in profits, and your Board of Directors and Shareholders will be pleased at the positive results.

It is important for you to know that in this era, Sales Forecasting, Strategic Planning and Projections will not work anymore as is. It is NOT business as usual. Such tools and activities will only work if Divinely inspired, because the *'grace period'* has ended. You must now go back to the basic principles of the Word of God to help you to become successful and grow from strength to strength. Biblical Economics teaches you how and when to invest, even in times of famine and disaster.
Your organization has the potential to be one of the most powerful forces not only in your sector, but also in the World Economy. The earning potential is great and the possible impact it can make on the lives and the quality of life for the peoples of this nations is endless.

Therefore, in the face of the adverse economic, financial and spiritual status of the world, and its capacity to make or break the society, what has your organization done to improve the quality of life for the nation?

It's not too late to make a change!

What To Do – What God Wants You To Do

The tables are turning and it is imperative that as a player in this economy, you take the decision to make serious and drastic changes in an effort to remain ahead of the game, and build the nation in the face of adversity.

There are numerous things that God wants you to do that can revolutionize the entire business sector wherever you are!

> ➢ Use the genuine Apostles and Prophets of God as Advisors in your business/company

> ➢ Have daily Devotions in your company

> ➢ Ensure that your company pays Tithes

> ➢ Ensure that you pay Tithes

> ➢ Do not encourage or allow yourself or your company to be a part of witchcraft

> ➢ Employ fair business practices at all times; do not oppress the poor, the fatherless and the widowed

> ➢ Assist in advertising Church events

> ➢ Sponsor events that bring Godly healing to a nation

➢ Pull away from sponsoring shows that promote sexual immorality, cults and other religions

➢ Cease promoting nudity as projects for helping the poor

➢ Offer discounted rates to Churches and Christian organizations

➢ Donate your used furniture to Churches – particularly to smaller or younger churches

➢ Fund Visions! Many people have a Vision, but don't know how to get it off the ground – ideas that can bring solutions to your business and to the nation

➢ Look into employing Christians and or investing in their Training

➢ Sponsor business seminars and conferences on Crime, Violence, Human Empowerment, Entrepreneurship & Small Businesses Development.

➢ Assist in setting up Publication Companies to help this generation of young writers.

The bottom line is simply this; do business God's way! In order to reap continued success you must seek to be a part of the Prophetic Move of God!

This New Move

This new move – new venture – will increase Advertising and Marketing for the company.

If this new move does not take place, then:

- ➢ Extortion will increase and run rampant throughout the nation

- ➢ Crime and Violence will skyrocket

- ➢ Visions will not come forward

- ➢ Loss of Profits for your industry/sector will be great

- ➢ Loss of Jobs will soar, and

- ➢ Sales will decrease dramatically

You must now look at having Pastors and Qualified Christian Counselors all filled with the Holy Spirit to be Chaplains within your organization. Psychiatrists do not know or refuse to acknowledge the truth concerning these matters and many of them are involved in the very things from which you would be trying to disassociate yourself.

You will need to cease your organization's involvement in Cults and cultic activities.

By including or involving God's Prophets as advisors to the nation – God would do and allow mighty things concerning you and your organization. These are some of the things God would cause to happen if these were implemented:

➤ Anointed Staff with God-given Visions and Ideas would come forward

➤ There would be a substantial and significant increase in Market Share and even Customer Satisfaction.

➤ There would be positive Cash Flow

➤ There would be continued success

Further Suggestions

The things of the world affect people – debt, greed, power, love of material possessions and luxuries, broken relationships, love of money, sexual lusts and immoralities – and people need solutions that will in no way destroy them. You have a responsibility to the youth of the nation, and you also have a role to play in promoting solutions before it is too late.

➤ You need to set high standards in your advertising, for example, in programs and commercials that either have high sexual connotations or blatant sexual antics, witchcraft and sin.

> ➢ Many businesses tap into the demonic realm and this needs to stop.

What does a person do with the God-given solutions for the nation? What part can you play?

If you desire to be a part of this new move, let Lyston Consultancy help you to achieve the success that God would have you to achieve, the way He ordained you to achieve it! God never fails, and with Him, neither will your business!

Chapter 2

BASIC BIBLICAL ECONOMICS

It is important for us all to know that the Bible is the ultimate handbook for life and carries a wealth of information on every issue of life! As you read this book, you may or may not realize that it is filled with solutions and hidden treasures! It is a valuable asset which can help each person, each organization or any nation, to live and be prosperous, healthy, wealthy and wise!

On a more in-depth note, 'Biblical Economics' is *"the study of how to use limited resources to satisfy unlimited needs and desires that come about as a result of human existence, through the application of Biblical Principles and Divine Revelation."*

Intrinsic in the application of Biblical Economics to everyday life is the importance of recognizing several things you must do.

➢ Obey Deuteronomy 15 regarding debt write-offs. *Verse 6 tells us, "…you shall lend to many nations, but you shall not borrow; you shall reign over many nations but they shall not reign over you."*

➢ Sow much, especially in the eighth (8th) Year and eat old produce until the ninth year until its produce come in, you shall eat of old harvest. Leviticus 25: 22

➢ Know the Principles When Lending To The Poor. Leviticus 25: 35 – 38

> Give more than your required ten percent (10 %). There is nothing wrong in giving more than ten (10) percent; you can give more according to the blessing of the Lord. Deuteronomy 16: 17.

Always remember that all things are controlled by God, including your riches! All in heaven and earth is His. He is the Head of all; He is your banker. He tells you what to do with your money, because your money is His! You are only the distributor; it is for Him and all riches and honor come from God!

According to I Chronicles 29: 17 know that God will test you to see if you will give to build his temple.

Biblical Economics On Poverty

No nation can effectively deal with poverty unless they apply Biblical Principles. Ephesians 6: 10 – 13 reveal that what you fight against or struggle with is not physical but spiritual. According to II Corinthians 10, it is also a stronghold. Therefore it is safe to conclude that poverty is not only a stronghold in the lives of many, but also spiritual in nature. You cannot deal with a spiritual problem using natural methods. In order to deal with poverty you must first deal with foundation of poverty. Jesus always taught His people the Biblical Principles of dealing with poverty. He reveals that Sin is the leading cause, and this includes:

> Robbing God of Tithes

➢ Witchcraft

➢ Idolatry (Serving other gods)

➢ Seeking other sources instead of seeking God first (Matthew 6:33)

➢ Restoring familial foundations (Malachi 4: 5 – 6)

➢ Justice for all

➢ Dealing with interest rates on a national level

➢ Companies' inability to abide by Biblical Principles to turn a nation

A nation's economy must be built on God's principles, not on man's. Further to this, handouts from various nations, tie the nation down in debt and cause the nation's valuable resources and assets to be given away to foreigners.

Those handling the finances of the nation must be holy. His/her life must be in line with Biblical Principles. (Look at Titus 1: 6 – 9)

God uses I Timothy 3: 13 as the main criterion for judging all leaders of and within the nations, whether secular or spiritual. This Scripture gives the main qualifying and salient requirement which those who lead you ought to have. God's people should run for office. All the necessary qualities for leadership are in the Scripture. These qualities will bring change to a nation.

Nehemiah 5 also outlines what the leaders were doing to cause poverty on a nation. God wants leaders who are anointed with His Spirit to bring reformation to a nation; only those with His Spirit - no other spirit. There is no way mankind can deal with the economy of a nation if God is left out of the picture. If you do that He will also do that to you. God is the One that gives increase and growth in a nation. No real growth can come about unless God is involved. If there is growth and God is not involved, it is going to fail and be uprooted by God. Only what is built on Biblical Principles can stand.

The first steps in addressing a nation's failing economy are as follows:

➢ Inquire of the Lord

➢ Apply the instruction given

➢ Check all foundational problems from the past, for example, things which leaders had done that need to be renounced

➢ Determine which spirits have legal right

➢ Break vows or deals that have been made with ancestral spirits

Having discussed earlier the importance of symbols, colors and signs, it is important to recognize that these things affect a nation as well. It affects the nation's finances and economy. For example, the symbols of Leviathan (Job 41; Psalm 74: 9 - 17), which is the alligator or the snake, on anything belonging or assigned to the nation, negatively affects the trade and finance of the nation. Further to this, Ezekiel 28 – 29 speak of the symbols that affect trade:

➤ The level of wealth of the rich versus the expense and debt level of the poor

➤ The extent to which pride has taken over the nation, its leaders and its people

Realize that when pride has taken over, people begin to see themselves as gods in business and in the nation. Get ready, because God is about to deal with this issue!

No One Listens To The Poor

Ecclesiastes 9: 15-16 says, "Now, there was found in it a poor wise man, and he by his wisdom delivered the city. Yet no one remembered that same poor man. Wisdom is better than strength. Nevertheless, the poor man's wisdom is despised, and his words are not heard."

Wealth commands attention. Money talks - people listen. Regardless of how good the idea is to bring change and save lives, nobody listens to you when you are poor. When a rich man speaks, even if it is foolishness, the media, the government - everybody gives attention.

When you are poor, nobody listens to you nor takes your word seriously!

As I have said many times, it does not matter how wise and anointed you are, if you are poor, no man will remember you. This is why Christians should not allow anyone or any circumstance to stop them from pursuing wealth, but in the right way.

Christians And Wealth

Many times, people paint a picture that Christians should not be wealthy, nor should they pursue wealth at all. But II Corinthians 8:9 tells us that Jesus became poor for us to become rich; and that can be both spiritually and materially. When we have wealth, we are able to execute God-given plans, realize visions, get involved in representational politics, without donors who have a different agenda. We can put forward real solutions to benefit all. Further to that, when we have wealth, then people will think twice before they try to make a name for themselves by ridiculing Christians. When we have wealth, we can sit at the table of decision and make real changes and a big impact. When we have wealth we can fund our own campaigns.

There are many, who unfortunately are among the poor, who are in fact sitting on gold and diamonds - solutions that can bring positive and lasting change. But having all this without the tangible resources to execute the ideas to show.

For example, if we say we have faith but cannot show the manifestation of wealth, then no one will take you seriously or want to give you certain access. When someone is wealthy, they are given certain access and opportunities that the poor have no access to. The rich man does not have to join the line or go through certain 'red tape'. His money is his password. The wealthy don't have to go through the rigid screening that the others do, nor are they subject to certain laws that govern everyone also.

Immigration problems don't affect the rich as they affect the poor. Most countries offer citizenship to the rich. In this world, money talks and nothing else matters! When a rich man speaks, respect is shown - even if he is speaking nonsense.

Many times, the poor curse the rich for being rich, but the poor must always make the effort to learn certain principles from the rich. The rich have learnt, to some extent, how to turn problems to profit! The rich stay in the company of their peers and support each other. I guarantee you will see more of the rich coming to the front line because they are unashamedly taking up global positions. This is why there is the need for more of the poor to become rich so they, too, can take their place and bring solutions to the table.

There are certain fundamental principles that the poor need to embrace. For example, they need to:

- ✓ Join chambers of commerce;
- ✓ Cut down on fast food and spend wisely;
- ✓ Make long-term goals and objectives;
- ✓ Start volunteering and work for the wealthy; and
- ✓ Before you curse them, pray for them and you received divine favor.

Stop focusing on what you don't have and start focusing on what you do have. God has already given you gifts and talents which can make you wealthy. You may think it small and insignificant, but nothing is so small that it can't create a future for us. If God allowed it for Bill Gates, Warren Buffett, The Matalon family, the Issa family and Michael Lee-Chin, then He can do it for you, too!

It is time for you to start a business, create jobs for others and contribute to the nation's economy and to the lives of others.

So, remember, if the Scripture says that no one will accept you, nor your decisions and intellect when you are poor, then it is time to get rich.

Biblical Economics On Giving

Throughout the Bible, numerous examples can be found concerning giving to God; and many of the men of God - David, Elijah, Abraham – proved God in their giving and took it a great pleasure in giving unto God!

Giving a seed of $10,000 to build God's temple will bring great blessing on your life. David gave three (3) thousand talents of gold and seven (7) thousand talents of silver totaling ten (10) thousand talents to build. The only reasons God gives wealth and riches are to:

> ➤ Build His Kingdom

> ➤ Fund the poor, the fatherless and widow

Once you obey you will never be broke!

God gives resources for man to administer, and He uses man as manager of His resources on earth. All resources belong to God and He will deal with any mis-management of His resources. For example, government ministers, Church leaders, businesses and individuals, God will hold them accountable. He holds them accountable because He gave man dominion over the things of the earth. He put man as stewards on the earth and so man is responsible for earth's problems.

God is always ready to use you as an agent if you are ready to seek His wisdom to manage His resources.

To be a millionaire, you must understand times and seasons according to Ecclesiastes 3. While you ought not to engage in numerology, you must recognize that numbers have great significance to God!

The number ten (10) for example, from a Scriptural standpoint, means '*test; prove*'. It is the number of divine economy and the diverse elements of it - God's eternal injunction. The Law of Tithe is an injunction. Ten (10) represents Tithe!

Numbers are very important to God, especially in regard to sowing. Learn about numbers and what they mean scripturally.

Always keep in mind, God will send rain for your seed! Sow in the ground and food that comes from the Lord will be rich and plentiful. According to Isaiah 30: 23, *"Then He will give the rain for your seed, with which you sow the ground, and bread of the increase of the earth; it will be fat and plentiful. In that day your cattle will feed in large pastures."*

It is very interesting that nations always increase taxes, which become a burden on the people, while ignoring Tithing, which would bring great blessing on the nations; it would also allow for a reduction of the increased taxes (to be imposed on the people) that were put in place to deal with economic shortfall. As a millionaire you must always watch this area and not make the same mistakes! (Read Nehemiah 13: 12 – 13)

According to I Corinthians 16: 2, Paul says,

"On the first day of the week let each one of you lay something aside, storing up as he may prosper, that there be no collections when I come."

Simply put, as a person prospers he/she should increase in his/her giving accordingly. Know that the more you prosper, the more you give and the more you give, the more God will give to you!

According to II Corinthians 9: 6 – 7, the measure in which you sow is the measure in which you will reap! If you sow without a limit, you will receive without a limit. If you hold back on God, God will hold back on you! Whatever returns you are looking for, that is the measure in which you must give.

The Scriptures state that God loves a cheerful giver, and His love will bring great favor! God wants to give His people a divine bonanza; meaning a source of wealth and prosperity, a large output or a mine, good luck.

As a millionaire, always help an Apostle or Prophet or any man or woman of God to carry out God's mandate. Let no one tell you not to do so, because there is a great blessing for doing just that. In I Corinthians 9, Paul outlined what he was entitled to receive. There are three (3) sources from which he would receive his financial support. Society dictates that those who render service such as a soldier, a farmer or a shepherd, should receive remuneration. The principles even apply to working animals like the ox that tread out the grain.

In I Corinthians 9: 14, the Lord commands that those who preach the gospel must be supported. Read Matthew 10: 10; Romans 10: 15.

The Book of II Timothy 2: 6, the hardworking farmer must be first to partake of the crop. But He must plow the ground first, before he reaps a crop. But if he does he will not receive the reward of a bountiful harvest. The hardworking, laborer will be rewarded.

Millionaires should in no way sponsor activities that involve perversion in any way! This will bring a curse to their organization. Anything you use your wealth to support, which is anti-Christ, or in any way opposite to God's ways and principles, will backfire on you and your organization. Ensure that you:

➤   Pay your tithes

➤   Obey the three (3) feasts

➤   Sow seed regularly to build the kingdom

> ➢ Help the poor, the fatherless and the widow

As a millionaire, you must keep in mind the premise of Luke 12: 13 – 21 and Proverbs 11: 28. Do not let riches and the blessings of God cause you to lose your salvation! Many are hindered because of this greed. Your mind must be focused on the things of God first.

Luke 12: 13 – 21 speak of a rich man – deemed the 'rich fool'. Verse 16 of this Scripture tells you that his ground *'yielded plentifully'* and this means that he made a large profit. The Scripture further tells you that the present structure of his organization could no longer deal with the massive growth. Hence, because of the blessings of God, there was need for expansion. However, with the massive expansion, there was no expansion toward God! He was not at ease because of the great wealth; no provision was made for his soul; no treasure was laid up in heaven, and God saw this act as foolish!

As you read verse 20, recognize that God is the One Who controls life! If death comes, it will come because there was no honor being given to God, nor was there any consideration being given by man to the laying up of treasures in heaven.

This rich man was expanding in the natural, but he was dying spiritually. God wants both spiritual and natural expansion regarding wealth. God wants you to be rich in both ways, and verse 21 clearly states what God means.

In Luke 12: 22 – 34 God is saying you should not worry about food and clothing. Life is more than that. The ravens neither sow nor reap; they have no storehouses or barns – God feeds them! How much more value does He place on you than on the birds.

God does not want you to worry about the things of the world! But instead, He wants you to seek the kingdom of God and all these things will be added – including wealth!

Verse 33, God says that the rich should sell and give – sow – seek out kingdom things first! Sacrificial giving for the needs of others assures you of the treasure that can never be lost.

The 'Rich Man' Seed

This seed can be sown as follows:

Matthew 12: 1 – 33   - $12,133.00; $1,233.00; $12.33; $33.00

Please note that Nehemiah 12 speaks of Government and Apostolic Rule. It is the number of God's Covenant. *'One'* (1) is the number representing *'power and authority.'* *'Twelve'* (12) is the number of *'natural creatures holding spiritual power in their hands. It is the number of government.'*

Why worry when you can give sacrificially. The raven can neither sow nor reap and God still feeds them. You are more valuable and you have the honor and privilege of sowing and reaping! There is nothing wrong with selling and sowing. Sow into the kingdom and lay up treasures.

For this seed of $12.33 God will also give you things to sell that you can sow - money bags, new investments, new businesses, new plans – money will always be flowing. No old business!

An investment in heaven means nothing can touch it; and that investment cannot fail. Other investments can fail, but not this investment! It also means that no thief can come near your investment – it is fully protected! Not even a bad economy and intellect can affect your investment – no one can give you a Cease and Desist Order for your heavenly investment!

The number three (3) is the number of the Godhead; the number of invincibility. Genesis 1: 9, 11 and 13 Conform, obey, imitate, likeness.

Thirty (30) – priest, maturity, service – Numbers 4: 3; II Samuel 5: 4; Luke 3: 23

Luke 16: 19 – 31 as lovers of money, the Pharisees looked upon wealth as a sign of God's blessing, and looked upon poverty as a sign of His judgement. Jesus teaches that material possessions are a trust from God to be used responsibly for God. God is calling those with wealth to repent and help others with their money. *'Dives'* is Latin for *'a man of wealth'*.

Proverbs 8: 17 – 21 tell you the benefits for loving God and seeking Him.

> ➢   God loves those who love Him

> ➢   Those who seek Him diligently will find Him

- ➤ Riches and honor are with God

- ➤ Enduring Riches and Righteousness

- ➤ Fruit that is better than gold, fine gold. (Fruit brings harvest, different types of harvests)

- ➤ Revenue is more precious than choice silver

Those who love God, He will cause to inherit wealth. He will fill their treasures.

- ➤ Proverbs 9: 10 – 11 speak of the benefits of fearing God! The verses speak of receiving wisdom, knowledge and understanding.

- ➤ In Proverbs 10: 27, it declares that long life will be added to you.

- ➤ Proverbs 3: 2 also speaks of peace that will be added, God is peace and He gives peace.

- ➤ Proverbs 8: 10 – 11 let you know that to receive God's instructions is better than rubies, and all things that a person may desire, cannot be compared!

- ➤ Proverbs 11: 24 – 26 state that generosity prospers a person.

> Proverbs 13: 11 declares that wealth gained by dishonest means will diminish; but that he who gathers by labor will increase.

Millionaires, wise men and government persons cannot worship God without a seed. As you look at Luke 2: 11, you will see that as the wise men came to see Jesus it is clear that they understood the Seed Principles and the Law of Exchange. They needed a blessing, so they presented their gifts to Him – Gold, Frankincense and Myrrh. (Read also Psalm 71: 10 -11)

In Isaiah 60: 6 – 7, God is blessing Zion for His purpose, and is using the unsaved to bless Zion! Likewise, God is raising up millionaires who will build His temple; only those who will give without reservation will be promoted in this season! It is the duty of the gentiles to bless Zion. The wealth is to build the temple of God.

In Ezra 1: 5 – 11, God stirred up His people to build His house. All those around them encouraged them with articles of silver, gold, goods and livestock, and with precious things besides all that was willingly offered to build God's house.

Isaiah 60: 12 reveals that any nation or kingdom that refuses to serve Zion, which is the city of God, will be utterly ruined! You need to give part of your money to build God's house.

What you must recognize as millionaires is that this kind of giving is part of worship. What it means is that all those rich, wealthy, wise persons who refuse to give to

God's work, are going to become bankrupt in the end time!

Isaiah 60 is the Scripture for nations and millionaires – for any nation or individual that:

> ➤ Pays Tithes

> ➤ Worships the true and living God

> ➤ Worships God with their rewards

> ➤ Abides by Biblical Principles in all undertakings

Look at the promises of the Lord.

In verse 17:

"Instead of bronze I will bring gold, instead of iron I will bring silver, instead of wood, bronze and instead of stones, iron. I will also make your officers peace, and your magistrates righteousness."
In verse 18:

"Violence shall no longer be heard in your land, neither wasting nor destruction within your borders; but you shall call your walls Salvation and your gates Praise."

In Isaiah 60, when the glory of the Lord is risen upon you, there are great blessings to be received. When the glory is on your life, the glory will bring great wealth, power and brilliance. God's presence through the power of the Holy Spirit will give you grace and favor. It is also a sign of His pleasure and acceptance of the offering and praise. The Hebrew word for the *'glory'*, is *'chabod'*. When the ark of the Lord, which carries the presence of the Lord, was in Obed-Edom's house for three (3) months, God blessed him and his household. So not only was he blessed, but all his family members were blessed as well.

Millionaires, VIP's, wise men must allow the presence of God to be in their house. Once they entertain His presence, all the blessings will come upon their household. When the glory is on you, even when darkness covers the earth via economic problems, disasters on the people and so on, the Lord will arise over you, His glory will be seen upon you. The Gentiles shall come to your light and opportunities shall come to your house. More sons and daughters shall be taught by you and nurse at your side. Glory and earthly wealth will also increase in every area your life.

Psalm 73: 20, Deuteronomy 4: 15 – 40 and Exodus 20: 4 – 5, let you know that as a millionaire you should not have any images in their houses or business places – whether governmental or private. It is idolatry!

If there are any images or statues in any form – male, female, animal or angels, know that God is a jealous God! To remain wealthy, you must obey God's instructions. Many people have all kinds of images – including images of Jesus on the cross! While you must remember His sacrifice on the cross, it is more important to remember that Christ is no longer on the cross! This is the symbol of hope you must embrace – He is risen!

You may have images as art work, collections from various countries. Your place of work and your home must be clean of these things that the Lord can dwell in your environment. Many people have ashes of dead relatives in your house – you are automatically turning your place into a cemetery. This will hinder your prosperity.

As Psalm 73: 28 admonishes, millionaires must put their trust in God, draw near to him, that God will declare all your works. As you see in Jeremiah 17: 5 – 8, when you trust God, there are great blessings. In addition to this, in accordance to the instructions of the Lord in Leviticus 19: 26, as millionaires you must keep away from divination. You will be brought down to nothing if you indulge in it.

The Power Of Color

All New Millionaires must know about the power of color. For example, you need to know what each color means, when to wear what color to various functions, how to know which colors will bring the blessings of God, and how God speaks to you using colors.

Did you know that God has a favorite color? His favorite color is blue! Below is a simple chart to give you an idea of the negative and positive meanings of each color. Here are some examples outlined in the following chart.

COLOR	NEGATIVE MEANING	POSITIVE MEANING
Black	Death Despair Defeat	Creation Creativity Rebirth New Possibilities New Life
Green	Jealousy *(The Green-eyed Monster)*	Life New Beginning Nature Prosperity
Gold	Low And Dim Yellow Streak Self-Glorification Pride Silence	Wisdom The Nature of God Prosperity Glory Wealth Rare Gifts

God will ask you to wear certain colors in different seasons for ministry and appointment. Even the color you paint your office or house matters. Obedience is key!

Chapter 3

DEBT

Simply put, the term *'debt'* has several different meanings:

> ➤ Something that is owed' (in particular – money)

> ➤ A state of obligation to pay something owed

> ➤ Under obligation to a person

A *'debtor'* is *'a person who owes a debt'* (especially money).

Debt is the leading cause of stress, frustration, illness and every other malady that one can think of, affecting the world today.

According to the Wycliffe Bible Dictionary, in the Old Testament a *'debtor'* was to be pitied. In fact, it was a mark of divine favor to be in the class of the lender.

God wants companies, the government, other organizations and leaders as well, to abide by the Biblical Principles to help those who are in debt. Failure to abide by Deuteronomy 15 will result in the organizations and leaders falling into debt as well.

The instruction of the Lord is that at the end of every seven (7) years you shall grant a release of debts, and this is the form that the release must take:

"... every creditor, who has lent anything to his neighbor shall release it; he shall not require it of his neighbor or his brother, because it is called the Lord's release. Of a foreigner you may require it; but you shall give up your claim to what is owed by your brother, except when there may be no poor among you; for the Lord will greatly bless you in the land which the Lord your God is giving you to possess as an inheritance ..."

Write off debts owed by the poor. Don't take away the poor's assets.

For companies and leaders that obey the Lord there will be multiple blessings:

> ➤ Increase in business

> ➤ Expansion to do business (with individuals or organizations)

> ➤ You shall not borrow (from individuals or organizations) but will increase to the top and take over other organizations if you obey.

Many leaders will fail to receive a blessing this year regarding debt write-offs because of their disobedience.

Consistent obedience to God's commandments will make possible a society in which all poverty will be eliminated by God's blessing. The key to eliminating poverty is obedience to God's word. Failure to obey means the poverty will never cease from the land.

Deuteronomy 28: 12 reminds you that:

"... You shall lend to many nations, but you shall not borrow."

I Samuel 22: 2 states that debtors, the distressed, and the discontented followed David's army.

Using the Scripture in II Kings 4: 1 – 7, about Elisha and the Widow's Oil as an example, when you are in debt and the creditors are coming, you must first:

➤ Cry out to the Lord (Jeremiah 33: 13)

➤ Seek the Prophet/Servant of God. By calling on the Prophets of God, he/she may be able to show you something that will create a miracle or tell you how to come out of debt.

➤ Pray for that miracle. The thing that looks like it is of no use may be the very thing that can create millions.

Realize that:

➤ The jar of oil was likely Olive Oil used for both cooking and fuel.

➤ In ancient days, Near East women were regarded as inferior. So this miracle by Elisha demonstrated God's faithfulness, care and provision for the outcast. The provision was in proportion to the woman's faith and ability to receive.

> Lack of Faith can cease the blessing of God in your life and stop the flow.

In II Kings 4: 1-7, God not just used the Prophet to create the miracle, but He used him to give the Prophetic instructions to release the woman from debt (which is bondage). Additionally, He uses the Prophet to release provision to the family; from this provision they would survive.

Debt sometimes comes about as a result of dishonored pledges and usury which lead you into financial bondage.

Miscellaneous Laws

Deuteronomy 24: 6 & 17 speak of the Miscellaneous Laws.

Israel owned a small milling machine to prepare flour for daily bread. Taking this bread as collateral on a loan was forbidden since the millstone would be taken away if the loan was not repaid; and persons would be left without livelihood.

> Don't use your livelihood as collateral for any loan; seek the Prophet who will instruct

> The high interest rate charged by bankers; seeking creditors cause great hardship on the people, as in Nehemiah 5: 1 – 11.

➢ The redemption period should be extended and every effort taken by leaders – especially in Real Estate – before foreclosing on the house of someone who is in debt. This is particularly so for those who lost their house with large sums of equity in it, simply because of *'bad credit'*.

Exodus 22: 25 – 27 reveal that lending money to God's people who are poor, and then charging them high interest rates would bring great suffering and is condemned by God. Asking also for collateral or security from the poor in order to grant them loans and then taking away their collateral for non-payment during a bad season is condemned.

When the poor cry out to God, He will hear and be gracious; and when God hears their cries and answers, it means that many lenders and creditors will be out of business.

In Psalm 15: 5, God says that those who are not guilty of usury and do not take bribes against the poor, shall never be moved. High interest on loans to the poor is prohibited. Any individual or lenders that conduct themselves by Biblical guidelines shall never be moved.

In Ezekiel 18: 7 – 9, God speaks about the danger of one who takes away the debtor's pledge. He says:

➢ Do not exact usury – do not charge high interest rates nor take any increase

➢ Do not oppress the poor. They are being taken advantage of by the rich

➢   Execute true judgement

If you obey God's Word then such persons or businesses shall live. However, verses 10 -13 say that if there is refusal to abide by this and you are found guilty, you shall surely die.

Bringing people into poverty, debt, and succumbing them to high interest rate cause great suffering for individuals, lenders and creditors. It will cause death – both natural and spiritual – those that are operating in a way that causes God's people to be in bondage, so much so that they cannot worship Him, will bring judgement on a nation.

For financial woes to stop, and for companies and nations to return to profitability, they need to restore to their debtors their pledge. That is, they would need to return the collateral of their debtors to them. This is exemplified in Luke 19: 1 – 10 when Zacchaeus had to restore to his debtors four-fold so that salvation could come to his house; and also that they would receive the benefits of salvation. Which include:

➢   Deliverance

➢   Soundness

➢   Prosperity

➢   Preservation

➢   Happiness

➤   Rescue

➤   General Well-being

God is calling those who have oppressed the poor to return four (4) times what they have stolen from them so that they – the oppressors – can themselves be restored!

Deuteronomy 24: 10 – 12 state:

"When you lend your brother anything, you shall not go into his house to get his pledge. You shall stand outside, and the man to whom you lend shall bring the pledge out to you. And if the man is poor, you shall not keep his pledge overnight."

Further to this, verses 13 – 14 let you know that:

"You shall in any case return the pledge to him again when the sun goes down, that he may sleep in his own garment and bless you; and it shall be righteousness to you before the Lord your God. You shall not oppress a hired servant who is poor and needy, whether one of your brethren or one of the aliens who is in your land within your gates."

Here's an interesting question. If God were to deal with sinners, who are indebted to God as they have dealt with the poor, what would happen? MAJOR BANKRUPTCY!

Debt And Health

Leviticus 27 reveals that all the Tithes of the Land or of the fruit is the Lord's. Once someone withholds his/her Tithes, he/she will be in bondage – which is debt. In order to come out of debt you have to pay your Tithes, and in addition to that **add** one-fifth, which is 20%, to the total of the Tithes. For example, if your Tithes is $10 then you would need to pay $10 + (20% of $10) = $10 + $2 = $12.

An interesting thing to note is that the number five (5) means '*serve*'. Everyone is serving something or someone, whether good or bad.

As leaders you must recognize that the greatest bondage that God's people are under is DEBT! You become a slave when the nation is in debt. It is so because what happens at the top affects those below. Debt significantly impacts:

> ➢ Employment

> ➢ Downsizing

> ➢ High Interest Rates

> ➢ Great Suffering

No debt can be reduced by physical management only. It will require spiritual wisdom to be debt-free, in addition to good accounting practices. These are especially important regarding:

> ➢ Saving Energy

> ➢ Re-structuring

> ➢ Re-organization

➢   Staff/Personnel Education

so that each person can be a manager of his/her resources, and lets them know the importance of money in conjunction with Biblical Teaching, such as Tithes and Offerings, as well as God's timing and way of doing business through:

➢   Tight Spending

➢   Monthly Budgets

➢   Not purchasing what you can do without (Brand Name Items vs. No-Brand Quality Items)

➢   Saving on overtime expenses

Understand that money has to come from somewhere to be spent. Education, regarding cost and debt, needs to begin from childhood. Schools also have the responsibility of educating students in this respect.

In order to come out of debt, people need to be taught how to fish not be given the fish at all times. That is the way to prosperity. Additionally, in order to come out of debt you need to:

➢   Watch overdraft

➢   Use Credit Cards wisely

➢   Seek financial personnel to explain Interest Rates to you

> ➢ Watch penalties on loans

> ➢ Determine whether it is wise to refinance home at the present time

> ➢ Sell or rent. For example, mortgages

> ➢ Make additional payments on principal - it is the key to coming out of debt

> ➢ Make a monthly Budget

> ➢ Seek the Prophet for instructions according to II Kings 4: 1 - 7 in order to get the miracle.

Debt And Forgiveness

Debt is an issue which brings a great deal of hurt, bitterness and unforgiveness, and has affected not only individuals, but businesses and nations. Matthew 6: 12 reveals that not only does God want you to have debt write-offs, but His people must forgive their creditors from the heart. They must forgive them for the wicked things they have done and for having taken away their possessions, due to the high interest rates these creditors imposed on them. Now look at Matthew 18: 21 - 35 concerning the unforgiving servant.

God wants you to use these principles:

> ➢ Have patience in hard times

> ➢ Extend compassion

> ➤ Release the person(s) or organization and forgive him of the debt

Do not do what was done in verse 25, and put the family in slavery, prostitution – bondage. Do not take away their goods as payment (as with foreclosure or repossession). Do not employ this method, because God is against this principle; it is part of the oppression and slavery; it is bondage. Through the bondage of debt sons and daughters (the next generation) were being placed into debt!

In Luke 7: 41, Jesus teaches the principle that the greater the forgiveness, the greater the love. This parable is one which shows the contrast of two (2) debtors. The total amount of the debt, the forgiveness of the debts as well as the contrast in the level of gratitude of both is clear.

In applying these principles regarding Simon and the woman, Jesus shows that one who realizes the depth of his own sin and the greatness of God's mercy, must look as this woman does, her love resulted from her forgiveness.

Matthew 18: 33 tells of the same compassion that Jesus extends to individuals, businesses and nations, and lets you know that you must pass it on so that you may receive more from God; and that it is especially so concerning fellow servants.

Jesus teaches how the spirit of unforgiveness – the torturers, which is literally the Bill Collectors – exacts its toll on your body, mind and emotions.

Every kingdom-minded person is advised to sustain a forgiving heart toward all other persons.

Debt And Interest Rates

God wants His people to know that banks and companies make large profits off us through high interest rates imposed on us by them, due to the status of our Credit Scores.

He wants His people to be conscious of Interest Rates before purchasing. Most of what you are paying back on our hire purchases and loans is interest! This keeps you in bondage. For example, let us do the simple math:

What is the Total Payback when you borrow $350,000 @ 8.5% p.a. Interest for 30 years?

Total Payback =
Total Borrowed + Interest On The Amount Borrowed

$$= \$350,000 + [(350,000 \times 8.5\%) \times 30]$$
$$= \$350,000 + \$892,500$$
$$= \$1,242,500$$

This is what puts us in bondage and you must now seek to be debt-free and to own rather than have a loan.

God does not want the wicked to suck out the blessings from His just people; He wants His people to live free of oppression and bondage particularly in the area of finance.

Remember:

➤ Do not be too eager to purchase! You will always be under pressure to purchase things quickly and on credit. Be mean in negotiations! You are under no obligation to purchase things on credit, feel free to wait! You may find you can get it elsewhere at a lower cost or on better terms. Further to this, there is nothing wrong with taking time to scrutinize what is before you.

➤ While you sleep, the wicked are always planning market strategies to

- Take away your money
- Put you in debt and bondage
- Add to your stress and worry

And these things will put you in further debt. Understand that that is the design and purpose of the system and that is why it is even more important to adhere to Matthew 6: 33.

➤ Debt freedom will reduce millions in medical bills, worry, anxiety, stress and pressure. (Matthew 6: 25)

➤ Never use your Credit card to purchase unless it is an emergency. This facility will get you into bondage. Recognize that most of your business transactions are designed in such a way that you will need to use Credit Cards. Remember that Credit Card companies are businesses also and they benefit more the deeper in debt you go. If

➢ you fail to manage well in this area, it will put you in bondage.

➢ Be careful of whom you give your Credit Card information when transacting business. Always check your Credit Card statements to ensure that you are not paying for one thing twice, or that you are not being forced to pay for something in which you no longer have an interest.

➢ Use checks or cash as far as possible when carrying out business transactions and balance your checkbook regularly. Look out for overdraft payments. Try to stay away from Overdraft!

➢ Don't get involved in quick-turnover money schemes. Ensure that you have all the facts, including the level of integrity of the organization. Many of them are pyramid schemes designed to take your money without delivering what was promised.

➢ Always seek professional and certified help including legal advice by Christian professionals before signing certain contracts. The fine print is hurting God's people, and only when you are sinking in debt do you realize what you have gotten into.

Debt And Mortgage Shopping

As a millionaire, you must always be trying to find ways to maintain your freedom from debt. There are several things you need to understand in order to stay out of debt when shopping for a mortgage.

1. Always find out about the various fees attached

2. Shop and compare the fees in the market

3. If you go directly to the bank you would eliminate much of the cost, the broker's fee, for example, and would receive more funds in hand.

4. Find out whose right it is to choose title companies.

5. Always check your settlement charges properly to see if there is a duplicate charge.

Interestingly, if the banks change their rules, the brokerage companies will be out of business. The banks are too stringent regarding credit systems. That is why people shop with brokers

Always remember that:

6. The borrower is the one who is paying all those involved in the transaction, don't be deceived.

7. Those that are involved in mortgages should do their own mortgages.

8. The key is to get someone who can process the mortgage

➢ Broker

▷   Real Estate Agent

9. If a person's credit is good, and they have the necessary papers, then they don't have to worry.

10. You should never sign over the deed for, or give away property to someone else for any reason, without ensuring that you are totally disconnected from it in every way. If you want to give away or sow property, try other legal options. Remember, if you are still connected to the property and they don't pay, *you* pay. You can, for example, rent the property until you are detached from all liability, and then sow it.

11. You should never give someone a gift if you get the slightest inclination that it could backfire on you. Give, but cut yourself from it when you sow and get proper documentation.

12. No one cares about your finances but God and yourself. You must put yourself first if you are going to be a financial deliverer. This is not a recommendation to be as selfish as you want to be, but be wise and understand that you can't be a deliverer if you haven't the resources to deliver. Everyone wants to make a profit from you. You need to make a profit for yourself.

13. Be wise in business, when you make a mistake you will pay, most of those who get you into that mistake don't care after they make the profit. Their job is to keep you in debt, so that you have

14. to come back to them, to put you into further debt and continue the cycle of dependency.

15. Let no one force you into business that you are not ready to deal with. All businesses carry responsibility, cost, and sacrifice. The higher you go, the greater the cost you pay – everything carries a price.

16. Choose carefully concerning the persons with whom you will transact business. Persons with integrity are hard to find. Pray much and remember that you are living in a society where it's all about the money and not about integrity!

17. It is always better to do business with those who pay tithes so that the money can be kept within the kingdom of God - keep it in the family. Malachi 3: 10.

Things You Need To Know About Debt And Financial Fear

➢ Debt is the number one (1) cause of Poor Health. It brings on stress which negatively affects the physical body.

➢ Debt brings bondage; it enslaves you to your Creditor

➢ Debt causes you to lack control of your finances

➤ The only way you can be free to focus on God and His work is to be debt-free

➤ Debt brings embarrassment

Things To Know About Financial Fear

➤ Financial fear is triggered by Debt and is among the biggest issues that every person faces.

➤ Financial Fear also fuels anxiety, stress, pressure and suicide

Jesus teaches us how to live in uncertain financial times without stress or fear. In Matthew 6 He teaches that Financial Fear is:

➤ Unreasonable (vs. 25)

➤ Unnatural (vs. 26)

➤ Unhelpful (vs. 27)

➤ Unnecessary (vs. 30)

➤ Unbelieving (vs. 31 – 32)

To deal with debt and financial fear you must employ Matthew 6: 33, and seek first God and the things of the Kingdom of God.

There are many solutions in the Kingdom. In fact, there are:

> ➤ Many mysteries

> ➤ Cures/Solutions

> ➤ New Ventures

> ➤ New Finds

The earth itself was created to be directly dependent on God to function. Anything independent of the Kingdom of God will end up in chaos and increase debt.

Righteousness is the number one (1) key to Debt Reduction, Prosperity and Blessings on a nation and its people. The mere fact that people have ignored God in their decision-making is a lack of righteousness, which has brought great hardship on nations.

According to Proverbs 15: 21 the word *'righteousness'* means *'the straight and smooth way'*. It also means *'what is agreeable and pleasing to God because it is right'*, according to Deuteronomy 12: 25.

Lack of righteousness will affect the growth of and prosperity of a nation. Proverbs 14: 34

> ➤ Corporate righteousness brings corporate benefits

> ➤ Righteousness exalts/promotes a nation in every aspect of prosperity

Psalm 89: 16 – 17 declare,

"In God's name we rejoice all day long; in God's righteousness they are exalted."

Promotion comes because of God's favor. You are given power because of God.

When you are in debt, the first thing the system should do is set up a system to reduce your debt. Currently, the systems set up are formulated to get you further into debt. You cannot afford to be controlled by credit systems. The fact that your interest rates are controlled by the credit system shows there is no compassion. All the creditors care about is their money, at any expense.

I remember that during a season I was sick, I went to the doctor and had no health insurance. Even before I could recover they were trying to get me into more debt. Creditors will call you and harass you to pay, without caring if you are recovering. You may not even be in a condition to work, but all they care about is whether or not you have their money. This is a wicked system and it proves that debt is bondage!

Recognize, though, that God is going to deliver His people from debt/bondage. What He wants us to do is live by His principles. A time is coming when no one will use the Credit System. Many more businesses will crash and God will implement His systems to replace this Babylonian System which has had His people in bondage.

Healing will begin, herbs and natural cures will be discovered which will put hospitals out of business. Additionally, pharmaceutical companies will be coming out of business. Also, banks will be out of business, other lenders will be out of business. God is now shifting from these heartless businesses persons

The loan sharks, lawyers, accountants, and Credit Card companies, will suck you dry with interest rates. God is now raising up Christians who are determined to walk in integrity, who are not just in business to make money; those who understand the word *'grace'*. You cannot expect grace from God if you are not extending grace.

God is not pleased with the systems/lenders and so on; there will be a change very shortly on a global level. Soon, the only system for and way of doing business that will stand in this end time is God's system.

Debt-Free: The Pathway To True Liberation

Today, as we know, many persons are going through serious financial problems left, right and center. Some are on the verge of giving up, others want to commit suicide. Even teens are falling under the pressure. It is a fact we see first-hand globally. Every category is being affected - lawyers, doctors, teachers, pastors, laborers - even some bankers who desire to live right are feeling it now. Many say, "We have fasted, prayed and given and things are getting worse." People are asking the question - 'Why am I doing all the things I should, yet things get worse, while my neighbors do not and it seems they are prospering?'

But people who fear and serve God can't live the way the world does. We have to build our lives on God's economy and totally rely on Him.

The fact is that the world's economic successes and rewards are coming to an end. They have run out of ideas and they are on the last round. Economists can't even make a proper forecast.

Many of us are being pressed to the limit, but remember that it is through the fire that we, God's people, are born which means in times of hardship, our hidden gifts, creativity and potential are revealed to us.

God wants to and is going to bless His faithful ones, but He wants us to be debt free. Only when you have become debt free do you experience true freedom. We must be wise with the resources God is going to give us. We have to start getting rid of the credit cards and start reducing what we owe.

He wants to bless us so that we can be the new lenders. Recognize that when we give to the poor, we lend to the Lord. Lenders call the shots and they decide the interest rates. There are those who are poor who we have neglected, but we need to feed them! (Proverbs 19: 17)

God is calling us to seek Him more deeply. Many are too busy, hence they cannot receive what the Lord has in store for them. He wants to give them greater insight for their lives. He wants them to be inventors and unlock the inventions He is waiting to give each one.

God's Entrepreneurs

God is raising up new millionaires, entrepreneurs with solutions and new ideas. The world is bankrupt of solutions. The world cannot do without the kingdom. Even Pharaoh needed a Joseph.

Your suffering also brings wisdom. Impatience is what brings us into debt and problems most times. So God is teaching us patience and giving us knowledge, wisdom and understanding at the same time. There are too many crafty people lurking out there waiting to rob you of your inheritance.

Many times, we will lament and say God is late. But He was before time, in time and on time.

Your suffering can also give you a greater revelation of who God Is. There are different attributes of God - different sides of Him for us to experience. If we had no problems, His varying sides and attributes would not be revealed to us. Some, in their sickness, have found Him to be their healer; others experienced His provision and, in their time of lack, have found Him to be provider.

When one faces problems and there seems to be no way out - high debt, bad credit scores - He can be the God of favor to such one. His favor qualifies you when the odds are against you. Even if you may be facing eviction, or your business is being auctioned or if you have been denied a student loan - there is always a ram in the bush.

Many times, we go through hardship for the glory of God. But recognize also that we go through problems in order to increase our faith. When our faith increases, our favor will increase. When our favor increases, our vision will increase. So, too, will our power and money.

Chapter 4

ABOUT MONEY AND FINANCIAL MATTERS

When you look on the systems that are set up to deal with the financial systems, it is clear that it all comes down to one thing – it's all about the money!

The systems which include banks and mortgage companies do not set up systems to deal with people with:

> ➤ Low or No Income

> ➤ Bad Credit – no fault of theirs

One thing about the system is that it gives no consideration to the fact that in life there are ups and downs and seasons of lack of knowledge that each person will inevitably go through. Incidentally, in order to acquire knowledge and wisdom, it is very expensive – it costs money too.

For companies to pull out your line of equity and add to their income, it's clear that it's all about the money. They will only want to invest if they will make a *'killer'* profit off you. The entire system is designed to make the poor poorer, while those who have the capital, manipulate, control and plunder them.

The System

What system is there for those who are bankrupt or are genuinely going through a difficult period and have late payments. There is no system that caters for that. If, for example, you have bad credit and you want to clear it up, it will cost you. The lender will disqualify you based on your past concerning your:

> Mortgage

> Utility Bills

> Credit Cards

and more

God is the Chief Lender, especially of life. With this in mind, should our lives for the present or future be based on our past? If God, our Chief Lender, operated in the way these institutions do, what would happen to the world?
If Jesus never looked past our mistakes and the sins of mankind, would there be forgiveness of sins; and what would happen to us all?

If many of the financial institutions were giving people the opportunity to get back on their feet, would the people continue to be in such bondage? No they wouldn't! They wouldn't because then, they would be investing in something that can help them to become the next millionaire!

The system is so set that it is based on your current financial situation. They should judge and evaluate you based on past matters. They would rather foreclose on your property than give you a loan to get back on your feet, so it's all about the money. When they do that you lose both your money and equity. They get richer; but God is about to round up a set of Christians to set up banks to help His people; or as the Book of Habakkuk says, God is going to allow the plunderers to be plundered. The game they play is to say you are a risk to investors, and then on that basis they increase the interest on you monthly.

Interestingly, investors are double standard in their operations; because they don't purchase or invest in property with their own money. Instead, they use the banks' main resource – which is our money – and in many cases no detailed checks are done on them.

The entire financial system was never set up to liberate the poor and the middle class it was set up for the big players, who plunder God's people, it is the system in the first place that lead the people into financial bondage. The devil knows that the moment he can keep God's people in financial bondage, then he will have the upper hand. You can do nothing without money. Only the favor of God can set us free. Once the devil gets people in financial bondage, this will keep them from paying their tithes and offerings and sow seed into the work of God.

The Social Security Number

This is the next control system. Once you don't have a number you cannot transact business. Is this the beginning of the anti-Christ system? Once you fail to produce this number, then the financial institution will manipulate and enslave you by:

➢ Charging you higher interest rates

➢ Giving you less cash out

➢ Gets you into a 30 year commitment – by the time you finish paying it off, you already pay twice the original value.

The system is set for you to be slaves to leaders. They will paint a picture to you that you are not at risk, when they know very well that if you are in default they will sell your property.

God wants His people to follow the principles of Matthew 6: 33, seek Him that He will give them wisdom to deal with these wicked plunderers. All businesses must operate with the fear of God; He must get His glory in all businesses, not man.

The greatest war in the end time will be in the area of finance. God wants His people's possessions out of the hand of the Babylonian systems! The Enemy will, for example, use the world systems to punish the Church that purchased its buildings through major companies on loan, as well as those Christians that God has placed in authority. For example, within the legal and financial systems in addition to the medical system there will be a quick evaluation of those they must be held accountable for being lukewarm and not to merely sit in a corner and watch! They must decide which side they are on – God's side or the Enemy's. A line is now drawn and they will be accountable for the knowledge they have received. Those that walk in obedience and faithfulness to God, He will promote them, that they may have their own businesses. Thousands of people will be jobless within the various sectors. There will be sellers and no buyers as a result of the great injustice. Many of these bankers' buildings will become churches and housing for the poor. They will be closing down. They will be begging people to take loans as the days of their wickedness are coming to an end.

They have not regarded God as the one who gives the power to get wealth – according to Deuteronomy 8: 18. God is going to counter many of their systems.

Dealing With Financial Matters

God wants His people to have money! He does not want you to be a servant to the lenders; you must be servants of God only, in accordance with Proverbs 22: 7.

Psalm 105: 37 and Exodus 12: 35 – 36 both reveal that when God delivers His people out of Egypt, He brought them out with silver and gold. There was none feeble among His tribes – no sickness, no poverty. They were financially secure and debt-free. They were no longer in bondage. For God's people to truly walk in freedom, He has to deliver them from financial bondage. While you are free from the physical Egypt, Satan has set up a financial Egypt to lock you into great debt to become servants of the lenders and enslaved to him!

According II Chronicles 10: 3 – 6, when you are in debt, it is a stronghold, and you can't effectively pull down strongholds if you are in debt. You need money to effectively fight the battle. In addition to this, intercessors cannot truly be effective in the fight against the Enemy of souls if they are in debt. Most of the intercessors in the Body of Christ are in bondage. You must be free to fight, and it is hard to fight with a yoke around your neck or a chain on your hand!

What Helps Or Hinders When In Bondage

Arrogance, rebellious ideas and bad attitudes toward prosperity and giving needs to stop! You need to pray that God changes the mindset of the people regarding giving to God's work. Recognize that:

> ➤ You are in bondage when your church building is owned by a bank; just as much as it is so with your homes, vehicles and other assets.

> ➤ You are in bondage when you can't survive if you don't receive one month's salary.

> ➤ You are in bondage when you can't carry out the work of the ministry or execute your God-given vision because of a lack of funds.

➤ You are in bondage when you can't stay in the presence of the Lord as the Apostles used to do, because of lack in the church for effective ministry – as in Acts 4: 32 – 37; Acts 2: 40 – 47; Exodus 35: 2 – 7 (here the leader had to restrain the people from giving).

Obedience In Giving

When you are obedient to give, then when God speaks to you, you will be in a better position to pull down strongholds. The greatest battle you are fighting in these last days is in the area of Finance for the Kingdom! If the devil can dry up the finance within the Body of Christ and more specifically, in the church, it will stop the growth of the Church and delay the vision. That is why He gives Christians a carnal mindset regarding giving. Giving is a gift, where whoever seeks that gift, must seek it in order to build the kingdom. It is for this reason that you must pull down the strongholds of:

➤ Disobedience

➤ Fear

➤ Wrong mindset regarding the Church

Refusal to give is against the knowledge of God.

The devil always attacks us silently in this area, as this is the greatest attack on the Church. Unfortunately, the intercessors that are carrying out warfare against Satan's forces have found themselves in a bind, because they are the most guilty of opposing the Seedtime and Prosperity messages. They pray the least (or not at all) for God to pull down the strongholds from all our minds, so that we may accept the Seedtime message, and sow in order to get the harvest God wants to release to us.

Unity cannot happen in the Church when poverty is rising. The deception is out! Pull down strongholds that the members will release God's money to fund the gospel – no negative talk in Church against giving; but instead willing hearts and positive declarations. Sowing seed is the answer to many prayer requests.

In addition to all this, Matthew 6: 10 – 11 show that ultimately, when you have money in abundance, God's Kingdom will come and His will shall be done on earth, as it is in heaven.

Matthew 6: 12 further speaks to us concerning forgiveness and debt cancellation. Only when you, the church, are debt free, will you experience the full Kingdom power! This must be prayed for daily, not only for yourself, but also for the Church, its leaders and members.

Additionally, Church leaders should declare Numbers 6: 22 – 27 over the congregation regularly – the Priestly Blessing.

"... The Lord bless you and keep you; the Lord make His face shine upon you, and be gracious to you; the Lord lift up His countenance upon you, and give you peace ..."

Borrowing

Deuteronomy 28: 12 – 13 show that God wants His people to stop borrowing. When you borrow, you join yourself to the lender; you are at the mercy of the lender. Remember, bondage causes suffering and pain.

God wants His people to lend to nations and not to borrow; that is a promise from God. When you heed the commandments of the Lord, He wants you to be the head, not the tail. The term *'head'* depicts *'authority'*. It is clear that He does not want you to be a servant to debt. You must pray that He will open to you His good treasure of heaven and give rain to your land in its season.

It is important to recognize that the term 'land' is 'the promised inheritance that God is going to give us'. Land is a blessing to build and plant. It speaks of increase and sowing. You need land! Once you are a son/daughter, you are entitled to land. Sons are heirs/successors to real estate!

Those children who are not legitimized are always sent away with gifts of movable prosperity, as it was with Ishmael and Hagar in Genesis 21: 8 - 21. Once you are the legal son, as Isaac was in Genesis 25: 1 - 6, then the Abrahamic Blessing extends to you – it belongs to you. You have a right to land, estate and the transfer of wealth. Additionally, always ask the Lord to give you authority in wealth, according to Deuteronomy 28: 13.

Sons are those with whom the Lord will establish His covenant, as in Genesis 17: 19; everlasting covenant with even his descendants also. If you are not recognized as a son, God will still bless you – as in Genesis 17: 20 – but it was with Isaac that God established the inheritance.

Inherit Land

In order to come out of debt and possess wealth, you must inherit land. Jacob adopted Joseph's two sons and gave them inheritance – land – according to Genesis 48: 5.
It is interesting to note that every seventh (7th) year was designated a year of release to allow the land to lie fallow, according to Exodus 23: 10 – 11 and Leviticus 25: 1 – 7.

Additionally, according to Leviticus 25: 8 – 55, Leviticus 27: 17 – 24 and Ezekiel 46: 17, the fiftieth (50th) year, which follows the seventh (7th) year, was to proclaim liberty to those who were servants because of debt and to return to their former owners.

Financial Peace

It is God's will for you to get financial peace and there are a few things you need to know in order to get there.

- ➤ Make God your source – Psalm 8: 4 – 11. If God is not your source, then as one problem arises, then everything falls apart. This is exemplified in Luke 16. This man was not depending on God.

- ➤ Know that God is your protection – Psalm 91.

➤ See God as your business partner. Let Him help you to make decisions. Matthew 6: 33

➤ Always see everything you own as belonging to God – I Chronicles 29.

➤ Always sow seed – Genesis 8: 22

➤ Always sow your way out of famine – Genesis 26 & I King 17

➤ Let all those who are around you, take financial responsibility seriously. For example, they must understand that everything has a cost factor.

➤ Each person must bear his/her own burden financially – Galatians 6: 4 – 5. They must know the value of money as well as its do's and don'ts.

➤ Don't venture into anything if you don't get any favor. Lack of favor will push you into debt.

Recognize that:

➤ God wants to take His people out of debt

➤ In this season people will have to learn personal responsibility, from working the land and eating from it.

➤ To walk in financial peace, you must walk in faith, according to Hebrews 11. Sow, Tithe and Walk in peace.

> ➤ Before you sign a contract – whether for a loan or to purchase anything – find out the current rate of interest.

> ➤ Always find out what your credit score entitles you to – including good interest rates.

> ➤ In negotiation always behave as if you can walk away. Don't negotiate in a hurry.

Additionally, there are other tools you can employ to get you financial peace.

> ➤ Always pay more on your loan payments than is required. This will reduce the length of time for the loan and it will be paid off quickly.

> ➤ Unforgiveness can cause us to be in debt – Matthew 6: 12. When you are in debt, you are in bondage; you are a slave. Forgiveness brings debt-freedom.

> ➤ Matthew 14: 22 – 33 especially verse 31 tells us that fear and doubt will sink you into debt. You have to keep your eyes on Jesus. There must be no fear or doubt – the *'boisterous winds'* in this Scripture speaks of doubt.

> ➤ God wants us to be debt free. His word in Romans 13: 8 says "Owe no one anything except to love one another, for he who loves another has fulfilled the law.

➢ Debt must be forgiven – Matthew 18: 23 – 35. Forgiveness brings blessings and helps us to be debt-free and to be out of bondage and slavery. Look at Luke 7: 41 – 42

You must recognize that the system was set up to keep you in debt by way of high interest rates! The enemy always uses money and loans to keep us in bondage.

Chapter 5

MONEY MUST DO GOOD THINGS

1 Timothy 6: 10 says, "For the love of money is a root of all kinds of evil, for which some have strayed from the faith in their greediness, and pierced themselves through with many sorrows."

There is nothing wrong with money itself. However, it is the love of money - the heart condition and motives behind the money - that is the problem. Money is a defense, it is supposed to do good things, and it is also to be used to create more money to win wars and transform lives for the better. When you have money, you have power and access. Money is even mentioned more than faith and prayer in the Bible - more than 2,000 times. When you have money, you can sit on boards in various organizations and run for political office, and when you speak nonsense, it will make headlines. People outwardly show you respect and treat you a certain way when you have money.

Christians should by no means be afraid to get money, as long as they are getting it legally; because if the kingdom of God is going to be effective in the end-time to transform nations, then we need money to impact lives.

Vow Of Poverty

Oftentimes, we hear people criticize Christians who have money, or those Christians who talk about money. But contrary to popular belief, there is no vow of poverty in the scriptures. Many have no problem when politicians or drug dons get money - whether legally or illegally; but as soon as a man of God begins to prosper, they have a problem - even when they get it legally. Money allows us to sit at the tables of influence so as to feed the poor, help by giving people scholarships, help university students who are struggling and cannot pay their school - most of them get locked out of the system.

God allows people to have money, not to sponsor evil. Money is for the purpose of doing good things (Isaiah 49: 50; Deuteronomy 8: 19; Proverbs 22: 16). That is why He allows organizations to make profit. We should not use our money to oppress the poor or give only to our rich friends, or use it to fund murders, rapes and sexual immorality.

Some would prefer to pay a witchdoctor to hurt someone, rather than pay for someone's doctor bill or buy them groceries or give a child lunch money for school. Don't allow money to become your master or your addiction - you should master money!

When man loves money more than God, then it becomes an idol to him, and they would also try to come against someone who is trying to make a living. Everybody must have an equal opportunity and an equal right to make money. So don't use money to put regulations in place to stop someone else from making money. Don't rob anyone of their wages and livelihood (James 5: 4; Jeremiah 22: 13).

Money Should Not Separate

Never allow money to separate you from God or from good friends. Money comes and goes, you never know which way the wind will blow. You may be a billionaire today and a pauper tomorrow.

Always pursue true riches, which are spiritual in nature - righteousness, Godliness, faith, love, patience. Don't allow money to cause you to betray those who trust you, including your leaders. Riches are so transient and the value changes. Earthly riches are only as good as its present value.

Wealthy people should be good stewards. The good we do today will bring eternal dividends. So find someone and begin to help them.

We must stop making decisions based on money only. For example, choosing political candidates either on how wealthy they are or how hungry they are for money.

Greed stops the flow of more money. Giving means we have conquered greed. So the moment our motives are/become right individually/globally, then we will see change individually/globally, and also the reduction of crime, violence and corruption, and people will start seeking to be in political offices - not for the love of money, but for the opportunity to serve their fellow man.

Chapter 6

NEEDED ... BANKERS WITH COMPASSION!

Matthew 18: 21 – 35

God is calling new people into banking and for bankers to change the way they operate so that those who suffer financial setbacks and crises will be able to maintain their integrity and status. Because of the Credit system in America, many people have gone through financial problems, so much so that when they recover they have it difficult to purchase anything!

The Credit System

The Credit System is of such that, someone, for example, will be late on their mortgage three (3) or four (4) times and that is used against them to disqualify them from refinancing, or from receiving home-owners benefits. However, some persons may be able to carry out a refinancing or get other home-owners' benefits at very high interest rates! This system has driven and continues to drive people to employ new ways to try and solicit help from others with good credit to help them to get a mortgage. Some then get quit claim deeds, and some don't. Some pay anywhere from $10,000 and more to get these transactions done! Some who make the mistake of doing such transactions in the first place end up losing everything!

God wants the banks to operate in such a way that those with bad credit will be given the opportunity to refinance once there is a valid reason for their credit going bad. The bank needs to have a committee of Counselors and Advisors and they need to create a system to help the poor with their credit. The credit system as it stands will have a major percentage of Americans owning a home in someone else's name.

Banks need to eliminate the use of a credit check to assess someone's eligibility to access a loan. The financial institutions will soon crash if they continue this way. They will soon be experiencing great decline in the number of persons seeking bank loans, and this will result in a famine among the financial institutions.

The oppression on the people is great, and there is the need for a change in the way financial institutions operate. These institutions need to operate according to God's principles. For example, realize that once you ask God for His forgiveness, then He forgives you. He does not carry those deeds or sins to the next year to appraise you! There needs to be a restructuring of the system because as it stands, it is not good for the country, it is only leading to fraud, lies and greed. Then money, not the capacity or ability to help people, becomes the sole focus!

There needs to be:

➢ Compassion in business

➢ Integrity in the system to carry out business transactions

The financial institutions, the bill collectors, and other such organizations must begin to operate with forgiving hearts in business. Once these organizations carry out debt write-offs every seven (7) years – as in Deuteronomy 15 – God would seriously bless these institutions; because, the way businesses operate today will cause many of them to be out of business very shortly. All who carry out transactions – dealers in furniture and cars, banks, mortgage companies, real estate organizations – will suffer as a result of this new paradigm shift in business.

Bad Credit

Any financial institution that begins to cater for the poor with bad credit will rise to the top, because God is looking for these institutions in order to bless them for helping His people by:

> Helping them to own assets legally

> Helping them protect their homes from foreclosure and their assets from repossession

> Presenting them with honest paperwork and helping them to upgrade their status in order to get loans.

> Setting up a system to hear their reasons for the crises they are in and helping them with solutions to come out of their circumstances free and clear!

That company would be blessed abundantly!

Such a company would need staff members who are not only qualified to bring solutions, but also able to operate with a great deal of compassion to effectively address the needs of such persons!

You cannot continue to operate business with a singular mindset - with just one thing on your mind – money, money, money regardless of the cost and whose expense! For many of these financial institutions, it does not matter who sleeps on the street; but you must recognize and accept that there needs to be a revisiting of the entire financial system!

Credit Scores And Interest Rates

It is an unjust practice to apply interest rates based on a person's credit information. Interestingly, High interest rates are not applied to the rich, even if they have bad credit, only to the poor. Solutions to this problem include the following:

> ➢ Have one set interest rate

> ➢ Have a three (3) - six (6) month grace period for those experiencing hardship and financial crisis

> ➢ Any adjustment to be applied in a period must be based on the season

> ➢ Once there is a case of foreclosure, all efforts must be made on both sides to recover assets, not to have *'sweetheart deals'* with rich friends.

> ➤ The lenders must have a restoration period as in Luke 19, to give back to those who were unfairly dealt with, in order to break the curse from their organization.

> ➤ Have a major cut on interest rates for all existing mortgages above 8.5%; so that people can own their estate, not live in bondage!

> ➤ All business transactions must be done using Biblical Principles, not to get someone poorer but to cause them to walk into greater wealth.

What Is Your Credit Score In Business

America's Credit Score System dictates that:

> ➤ 500   -   Low

> ➤ 620   -   Average

> ➤ Over 650   -   Good

As you look at business, you have seen where business owners use a person's Credit Score to determine if an individual is qualified to carry out business transaction. However you must recognize that this system is designed to oppress the poor and has many flaws.

In order to carry out certain business transaction, businesses charge high interest rate if they find that someone has a low score. These organizations do not factor in the qualitative aspects of the credit score such as a period of hardship! They don't do that because the Credit System was developed using anti-Christ methods, tools and procedures and is designed to keep poor people poor and increase the wealth of the wealthy – more so to control the wealth and its distribution!

> Are these companies paying Tithes (Malachi 3: 10)

> Are these companies sowing Seed/Donations (Genesis 8: 22)

> Do they appear to the Lord of the 3 Feasts yearly

> Do they honor the Lord with their First Fruits/Increase (Proverbs 3: 9 – 10: Exodus 22: 29 – 30)

> Do they give Debt Write-Offs every 7 years

God gives grace because you are in an era of grace! Why not give grace to all customers and persons with whom you do business!

If businessmen don't make a change in the way they operate, God is going to use the same system on them – which means that many will not qualify – great businesses will have a fall in sales. The presence or the grace will no longer be there; the glory will be removed from them. God gives the power to get wealth!

To repossess something from someone who has been a good customer over the years will not bring blessings upon a company. God prefers that you work out something with your customers, to help them get back on their feet and continue being good customers which, as you know, is beneficial to your business – there must be compassion in business.

The real question to ask is, "Are these companies' Credit Scores in good standing with God?"

Loans

In an economy that was set up by Old Testament Law, loans were set up for those who would undergo financial problem, poverty, stress, especially farmers who were involved in agriculture, to help people come out of debt and financial problem.

God always has a guideline for us to follow on how to deal with loans, especially concerning widows. God did not want His people to follow the commercial loan system set up by Babylon to bring His people into bondage. God gave the guidelines regarding loans in Leviticus 25: 35 – 37 and Deuteronomy 15: 7 – 11.

God does not want His people who are involved in the Loan business to charge His people and poor Christians. They should instead look at extending favor to these persons by charging low or no interest on loans so that they can become debt-free. Christian Loan Organizations and personnel cannot expect to operate the way the world operates and call themselves Christians.

The Biblical Laws on loans speak of releasing debts every seven (7) years! Additionally, it also speaks of freedom from slavery after six years of service, according to Exodus 21: 2 and Jeremiah 34: 14. Are you abiding by these principles?

Additionally, Biblical Principles concerning land found in Leviticus 25, state that the land that was taken away because of debt was to be returned to its original owner.

The Tax Policy

As it stands, America's Tax policy is not tourism-friendly. It is too expensive for those who are not citizens or residents. Many of those who fall outside those categories are major contributors to the nation's development and growth. Such persons have much to contribute by way of business ventures, projects and more. The tax must be reasonable so that foreigners will want to do business with the nation.

Now, a big part of the problem is that the Real Estate market is 'unfriendly' as it concerns foreigners. Once this changes then it will attract foreign investors and bring significant benefits to the nation. Land tax is particularly high and this will deter foreign investors.

The Insurance Systems

There is urgent need to look at the Insurance Systems – Health, Life, Vehicle, and Home Owners' – all kinds at all levels. As it stands, it is too expensive and particularly unaffordable to the poor. Today, even those who are affluent find it difficult to afford and this can lead to serious health issues within the nation.

Chapter 7

BUSINESS

An organization does not sustain on the building or the size of the building. An organization is built and sustained by people – the greatest investment any organization can make is investing in people by building them up. Jesus demonstrated this by training disciples. He empowered them with authority, to carry out the organization's mandate by nurturing and building up personnel. Many organizations are finding themselves in trouble now because no great emphasis was being placed on training and building up staff members and strengthening the organization. They spent a great deal of money on:

➢ Marketing The organization

➢ Developing Physical Property

➢ Developing Strategic Plans To Increase Sales

However, minimal was spent on the most important aspect of the organization – the people!

If you want to be successful in business there is no huge secret to real success – use Biblical Principles!

Let us recognize:

> God is looking for business people who are not in business only for the money, but also genuinely have the client at heart.

> Business people must do their business with compassion – not just for the commissions they are getting.

> God is looking for business people, who will do what it takes to protect their clients not just for one moment, but throughout the entire transaction and relationship.

> The business sector is being devastated because of the unjust business practices and greed. Greed is the root of the problems in business.

The questions then become:

> Is God getting His portion from the big business deals?

> Does God have a place in business?

> Do you remember that it is God that gives the power to get wealth?

> Why withhold key information from the customers? For example, their rights and the best way to transact the deals. Instead organizations

carry out the transactions and down play the fine print which is designed to snag the customer!

When businesses function in such a way that it brings pain or hurt to the innocent and the poor, there are consequences that will be meted out by the Chief Businessmen – the Chairman which is the Father, the President which is the Son, and the Chief Operation Officer (COO) which is the Holy Spirit!

Business people must recognize that making profits at the expense of others by ripping people off or deceiving them will bring them profits that will not last and consequences that will!

Profit

This is a term of great interest and can be defined in several ways:

> An advantage or benefit

> To obtain advantage or benefit

> Progress or advance

> Financial gain or excess of returns over outlay

> The positive balance remaining in a business after costs have been deducted

You will see several things as you read Isaiah 48: 17:

➢   It is the Lord that causes and teaches you to make profit.

➢   God is the One who guides you in the right direction, that you may be able to make profit

➢   It is God that has caused you to learn that you can make profit

➢   It is the Lord that gives you business ideas to make profit.

➢   God gives understanding

➢   For further profit from that profit, you must sow 10% from that profit.

Genesis 26: 13 reveals that there are three (3) stages of profit that God wants us to make in business.

➢   Prosper

➢   (Continue) Prospering

➢   (Become) Prosperous

Now for you to move from one level to the next in business or ministry, you must be willing to do what was done in Genesis 26: 12 – to sow that you may reap that one hundred-fold blessing.

According to verse 14, Jacob was then making large profits – so he could increase in business – in flocks, herd, great number of servants. You too will see your blessing multiply so that you may expand in His riches – in assets and resources.

For you to make profit you must understand that ultimately, it is the blessing of the Lord. (Deuteronomy 28; Genesis 26: 12) Now to maintain your profit you must always pay your Tithes, according to Malachi 3: 10 – 11, in order to prevent the devourer from eating out your margin. Remember, your tithes are your insurance premiums for you and your assets to stay protected.

It is extremely important for New Millionaires to know this - do not seek to make profit by dishonest means! Ezekiel 21: 12 – 13 explains. Making profit dishonestly is a sin against God! This includes:

> Taking or Paying Bribes

> Shedding Innocent Blood

> Engaging in Usury

> Lending money at exorbitant rates

> Setting Interest rates way above the law

> Engaging in extortion

> Getting money through any other illegal means

According to Isaiah 22: 2, it is the duty of God's servants and prophets to judge those who make profits dishonestly.

Isaiah 2: 14 – 15, you must understand that a time is coming when the Lord will judge those who carry out this act. Exodus 22: 9 tells us – don't oppress strangers.

Exodus 22: 25 tells you not to lend God's people money at large interest rates so that they suffer. It is a sin against God. Don't be like the wicked money lenders.

Luke 9: 25, Matthew 16: 26 and Mark 8: 36 – 38 tell you that it does not profit you to gain the whole world and lose your souls. The greatest profit is to ensure that your soul is alright and you make it to heaven. Don't lose your way and your soul for wealth and riches.

According to Acts 16: 16, I Samuel 28: 3, and I Samuel 28: 7, God doesn't want you to make a profit through divination or fortune-telling!

In the book of Acts 19: 21 – 41, there were great profits made and given to the craftsmen. The Greek goddess, Diana, means love and fertility. People are making millions from the sex trade. They also worship sex, sell millions of related products and engage in prostitution, homosexuality, lesbianism, sex changes, sex-related clubs, games, and pornography. Millions are being made from this trade.

In Acts 19: 25, you will see a lot of people were having their prosperity from that trade. They were making large profits from making sex images and objects, as well as statues – not only in Asia, but the entire world in the name of Diana. God wants His people to get them out of business; the profits that they are making are drying up God's Tithes and offerings. They are being used to fight against the church. The spirit of the anti-Christ uses it to fund their mandate.

You need to attack this trade that is making millions, bringing curses on the earth, breaking up Christian families and causing hardship!

This verse in the Scripture also helps you to see that not all prosperity is from God. For most countries their economic growth is as a result of their offerings to the goddess of love and fertility, Diana. These nations make millions in profit from their tourism industries. Many use casinos as a disguise to carry out this trade in their countries. But while they will boast about growth, what is the basis of their growth?

Because of the fear of losing their prosperity trade, they oppress Christians and the churches in their country. They will set zoning laws in an attempt to stop the Church!

Marketing and media companies are making millions from that trade also through advertising. The movie industries are raking in billions! Where do all these profits come from; and where do they go?

> Corrupt Politicians

> Buying weapons illegally

> ➤ Fraudulent Real Estate Deals

> ➤ Perversion of Justice

James 4: 13 – 16 is imperative, for those who are boasting and making plans to buy and sell and make profits – without consulting God. No one knows what will happen tomorrow; so God must be first and foremost in your life. You must always say, *'If the Lord wills.'*

Margin

Now as you read Luke 19 and Matthew 25: 14 – 29, they reveal that the Kingdom of Heaven **_must_** necessarily be operated in a business-like manner. God desires to make profit, increase on what He gives you. He wants you to handle your resources according to Luke 19: 13 – do business until he returns. Now it does not matter the nature of business whether secular or religious. There is a principle to be followed. God is looking for double returns on His investments; He is looking for interest! He is not looking at the amount of stock or flock you have in business or in His house. What He is really looking at is His margin, because this is where you see your true profit being made.

A smaller company has the potential to make a larger profit than large companies based on the volume and the margin. Margin refers to the percentage increase made. A church with 300 members can make a greater margin of profit for God than a church with 25,000 members. For example:

The basic sales definition of the term *margin* is *the difference between the selling price of a product and its cost, the percentage of markup.*

In investments, the money or security that a customer deposits with a broker when buying securities on credit; it is the amount that a customer deposits when buying or selling a futures contract.

Now let us look at margin in the Bible. In the Book of Judges, Gideon was called to raise up an army. There was a total of 32,000 - in business many stocks; and in ministry, many flock (a mega-church).

In business, you may have a lot of stock, but not much value. In ministry you may have a large flock that is fearful, as in Judges 7, and not producing, not making profit on what is given to them.

God Looks At The Margin

In Judges 7: 4, the numbers fell from 32000, to 10,000 and after the test was given, the number fell from 10,000 to 300 according to verse 6. Only 300 made it; God chose 300 to fight and this revealed the margin, because Gideon's 300 yielded a greater profit than the 32,000 or the 10,000 would, as the 300 totally defeated the enemy.

The markup is key and the margin is what gives you the profit. If all God's people started to have a cost reduction from their bills, and all cost related to get a bigger margin then they can give God more. They will be blessed and will walk in great wealth. This is earning extra by reducing costs.

Cost-Cutting And Resource Management

You need to make a greater effort to manage your resources. As new millionaires you must realize that whatever you save puts you in a position to give more unto God. That means that you will have a greater investment and therefore a bigger harvest.

For example, if your electric bill is *$120* monthly, do what you can to cut it by *$40* so that you only pay *$80* monthly, and sow that *$40* into the Kingdom of God. The number '40' means *'dominion.'* That $40 seed can bring you into multi-million dollar status!

Bulk Purchases

Further to this, even churches must cut cost and save to sow more or win more souls, give God more, not the unjust! Always remember that God does not tolerate wastage. All resources must be exhausted before you get overdraft.

It is always cheaper to do things in bulk than it is to do it in small quantities at a time. It is oftentimes better to buy in bulk – food, clothing, shoes, gas, even vehicles. It's wise also to cook in bulk, because these things will reduce cost significantly! Purchase gas in bulk. By filling your tank it turns out to be cheaper than buying a little at a time.

Better Management For Greater Harvest

The greatest investment you can make is to invest in the kingdom. So as you cut costs, you will have an opportunity for greater yield. Here are some examples:

> ➢ Cut down on clothing and shoes purchases in order to give, and you will even receive a more profitable harvest.

> ➢ Part of a ministry's production management responsibility is to ensure that God gets the full extent of all operational costs. For example, the Radio/Television Ministry carries a significant cost. If there is no sponsor, ensure that you recover the cost by selling the tapes of either the Broadcast or of the Message itself.

> ➢ Both your message CD's and tapes can be turned into a book, which will sell and go before you to open doors for you. God wants us to be cost conscious and efficient because in running our operations, there should be no wastage in the ministry. Everything must be done carefully and with wisdom throughout the operation.

> ➢ Always have two accounts – one from which you pay your bills and the other from which you sow your seed. Always pay your ten percent 10%, your Tithe according to Malachi 3: 10 and try to send another 10% to cover your family for your family.

➢ Always keep records of what you receive and what you pay out as donations. It is very important for record-keeping at any level – individually or corporately.

➢ Ministries must know who their top ten (10) Tithers are. Likewise, other organizations must be able to identify their top ten (10) customers, supporters or donors, and they must be treated differently.

Now, God judges when you have the little to see how you will manage the plenty – Luke 16:10

Chapter 8

MONEY MANAGEMENT IN BUSINESS

The Management of your finances in business is the most critical element and the decision you make can either make or break your business!

For someone to manage money properly, he/she must first seek the wisdom and guidance of the Holy Spirit, who is the Chief Advisor to our success financially. The Holy Spirit will unction you in terms of How to manage your money properly, especially when you are operating on a tight budget.

For example, what would you do in a situation when there are many bills to be paid, in addition to other expenses and salaries, when you do not have enough to cover those bills and expenses?

You will need to make every effort to allocate or *'spread out'* your funds according to the urgency of the bills in hand and pay the most important bills first.

> ➤ Check the dates of the bills to see if there is any grace period.

> ➤ See if there can be any arrangement with any of your creditors to pay a part of the amount so that the balance you have can be used to address some, if not all of the other bills you have in hand.

➢ Always call your creditors to see what arrangement can be made when you are late to cut down interest. Communicate with them that they will know you are facing a cash flow or financial problem.

➢ Try to be courteous, because they have the key! Make friends with them; they will eventually advise you of some very important opportunities that are available of which you were not aware.

In every difficult situation, there is always a way out. Additionally, you need to pray for the Favor Of God (FOG) daily, with business partners – anyone with whom you transact business.

➢ Fast and pray! The Esther Fast is recommended for great favor!

➢ Sow seed from everything in times of difficulty!

It is also imperative that as soon as financial difficulty arises, you need to inquire of God the nature of problem, what is its solution, and whether the gates are unopened as a result of not tithing or not sowing, for example. Maybe your record or bookkeeping is not in order. Maybe there is a curse, or someone in your household or someone connected to you in any way, that has messed up or sinned. Maybe witchcraft has entered the equation or you might be knowingly or unknowingly using your money to sponsor sinful activities. It could even be as a result of adultery, fornication, lack of integrity, wrong staff employed for the positions, or simply the need for a good, honest accountant!

For you to run a business efficiently there must be an anointed financial person who has the prophetic insight to help your organization financially. They must be able to put a plan in place to deal with Cash Flow Problems.

You might wonder, *"How do I rectify the situation quickly if I don't have that person in place?"*

You need to pray and ask the Lord to either direct you to that person or direct that person to you!

> ➢ They must be strong in the area of Administration particular in the areas of Financial and Operational Problem-solving! This will help to keep your company afloat and on the way to prosperity!

> ➢ They must be able to make quick, on the spot decisions in a crisis, including whether or not the business should advertise, where to do it in order to propel greater increase in sales.

All of these are critical decisions!

You will also need to decide whether or not the principal will accept salary during crisis.

Money And Prosperity - Zechariah 1

God is gathering His people to equip them in the areas of wealth to finance His work on earth! He wants to raise up those individuals in the Body within the local church to fund the vision. The vision cannot be funded without money and you must realize that each of us is born for a purpose! It is therefore critical that you find out:

➢ What is my purpose and what are my gifts and talents? (Matthew 25: 14; Exodus 35 – 36)

➢ Where should I go to serve with my talents? (Deuteronomy 12; Deuteronomy 28)

➢ Where should I go to get my purpose, gifts and talents developed? (Ephesians 4: 11 – 12)

➢ Under which vision should I line up? (Deuteronomy 12)

In our quest to identify and fulfill our purpose, you must also understand that:

➢ God is the one who places you where there are vacancies.

➢ He knows where is best for you to be so that you can be utilized for success and for His glory.

➢ God does not place you where there is overstaffing. He places you where the needs are for His will and purpose; both for your life and where the vision requires it. Remember that the entire vineyard belongs to God and He is the HR (Human Resources) Person that deals with placement!

Divine Placement

There are many persons that God wants to use in the Body of Christ to the fullest extent, but they are in the wrong organization. That organization has no vacancies for what God has placed in them and so, not only are they under-utilized, but that organization is now overstaffed and not able to realize the vision that God has placed in the visionary for that organization. As a result they die spiritually, without even realizing who they really are and what their assignment truly is in order to fulfill God's purpose on their lives!

God wants to place His people strategically, but they are not walking in obedience! They would rather become a part of what they see with their natural eyes and not paying attention to what God wants them to see with their spiritual eyes!

Now you must understand that God blesses you because He wants you to be a blessing to others. In the same way that God gives you spiritual gifts, you must understand that the gift of Giving/Helps (I Corinthians 12: 28), is a gift given by God for the purpose of financing the His Work! What it means is that not everyone is called to Prophesy or has been given the gift of healing, for example, but their gift may be to give to the Work of the Lord – to finance the spreading of the Gospel! (Romans 12: 3 – 8).

Now if a person has the gift of giving, then God is going to bless that person with riches so that he or she can serve God with it by giving to His work. Understand that by giving to the work of the Lord, that person is serving God; and as a result, God will increase his or her gift by adding other gifts if they remain faithful! For example, if a person with the gift of giving (gift of helps) remains faithful, then God may reward him/her with the gift of leadership in addition to that. This will enable him/her to acquire more businesses, new contracts, more or new doors being opened and new ideas, which would bring about increase and garner millions and even billions into and for the Body of Christ! All this so that there will be no lack to carry out His work! Further to this, persons will also be able to offer more employment to God's people so that they won't need to struggle or go through a hassle and be distracted from doing the work of God and ultimately they too will prosper!

God wants the Body to pray for Him to raise up and send people with the gift of giving in the end time to fund the Work!

It is interesting that the gift of giving and other gifts such as leadership, are the most overlooked gifts in the Body, and they are the gifts most needed in the Body of Christ. It is the duty of the church to pray, identify and equip people for the task ahead. Not everyone will be blessed with all the gifts, but all the gifts are related and they need each other to function properly. (Romans 12: 4 - 5) One body in Christ!

God Wants A Healthy Body

The only time the Body of Christ will walk in power and abundance is when all the gifts start to operate together. When that happens, then the Body will function without '*blood clots*' and without diseases. Instead, it will function healthily with no problems.

The Body as it stands today is malfunctioning because all the body parts are not working at peak performance.

All parts need to be present and functioning, and it is the role of the Apostles to get all the Body parts functioning so that there can be perfection, dominion, health, power, that the Body can become unbeatable – then the enemy will no longer be successful with the '*Divide and Conquer*' strategy against the Body of Christ.
Only when Zion's entire Body parts function will true prosperity return.

Romans 12: 8 tells us:

"*He who exhorts, in exhortation; he who gives, with liberality; he who leads, with diligence; he who shows mercy, with cheerfulness*"

The word "*liberality*" means "*free giving; freedom from prejudice; munificent; generous; bountiful*".

Only when the Body functions as one will people walk in the '*more than enough*' authority and dominion. The Apostles realized this, as outlined in the Book of Acts. They realized that they could not be effective unless the gifts functioned as one – all the gifts! That is why in Acts 2: 42 – 47 and Acts 4: 32 – 37 or even in Acts 5, as the people sold their possessions and laid it at the Apostles' feet there was no lack among them. They were united, they were together and on one accord and they had all things in common.

By reading Zechariah 1: 15 – 17, you will see that God is zealous for Jerusalem and Zion. He wants you to repent as He is ready to extend to us His mercy! He declares that His house shall be built! The term *'built'* means *'constructed, founded, set up, obtained - children, family, city, house, temple room, gate, altar'*. To build up something – anything – takes money! You cannot build without finance; even to build for future generations!

David, when he was about to pass on the plan for the temple to his son Solomon to build for future Generations, He gave out of His personal possessions to build! God is looking for His people to give great wealth to build!

He says in verse 17 that:

"... My cities shall again spread out through prosperity; the Lord will again comfort Zion and will again choose Jerusalem"

That means He will bring upon His people peace as well as relief from poverty, sickness and sin.

Here are some Scriptures of which to take note.

Isaiah 40: 1 – 2   which speak of spiritual warfare and that the Lord will pardon us and give us double.

Isaiah 51: 3   which speaks of *'Comfort'* (See also
Psalm 23: 4)

Isaiah 14: 1 – 2   which speak of how God's people will rule over their oppressors

Zechariah 2: 6 – 12   which speak of the future of Zion and of how God will take and give to His people. The verses also speak of the fact that those who plunder God's people will themselves be plundered.

Psalm 102: 16 – 17   which show that God will hear the prayer of the destitute

Chapter 9

THE BOOK OF LUKE

Jesus In Business And Finance

The Book of Luke presents Jesus as the world Savior and light to the Gentiles.

Now if Jesus is the world Savior (Luke 2: 32), then He is so in every area, including where there are obstacles in business and finance, and it means He has the answers to world issues!

The Book of Luke contains Jesus' encounters with rich businessmen and tax collectors, concerning the Kingdom of God and how they should follow after Him, without their wealth becoming an obstacle that would hinder them from entering the Kingdom. He also lets them know that their wealth would be valuable to the Kingdom to establish God's rule on earth – to help the poor, the fatherless and the widow.

Jesus took His ministry to the next level by starting to minister to businessmen and entrepreneur about the Kingdom of God and how they were to operate.

The Businessmen And Christ

Upon reading the Book of Luke you will see that Jesus went and ministered to the Chief Tax Collector, a very rich man by the name of Zacchaeus. He, like all other

Tax Collectors, was considered a social outcast and was despised because He co-operated with the Romans.

After Christ ministered to Zacchaeus, he gave half of his goods to the poor and vowed to return fourfold, anything he had taken by unscrupulous means!

This Scripture proves two (2) main things:

1. Jesus' mission was and is to seek and save the lost, without prejudice.

2. The first key to prosperity is SALVATION!

"Salvation" means *"rescuing, releasing, liberation, soundness and prosperity."*

There are many such rich persons who are having a change of heart for what they have done in the past. They want to obey the Law of Restitution (Leviticus 6: 1 – 5; Numbers 5: 5 – 7), having robbed others and desire to give back fourfold.

Trade And Interest

The Book of Luke speaks also of the principle of Trade and Interest. This principle escapes many as a principle of God! However, the Kingdom of God is also about Trading and Interest, and it is illustrated in Luke 19: 11 – 27.

Whatever God gives us, there must be trading and interest in return – our God-given gifts and talents must be involved in trade and interest! As God allows us to use our gifts and talents to minister to others, they in turn receive the ministry and yield themselves to God who gives them salvation. As a result, souls are added to the Body of Christ and the interest is added to our heavenly account – the full and final reward will be issued when we go to live with the Lord eternally. Notwithstanding are the major blessings we receive on earth as we use our gifts and talents for God's purpose.

Even in planting a Church, there must be interest!

God works with the number ten (10) regarding business. The number ten (10) represents the Tithe. It also represents God's economy. (Luke 19: 13) So if you should employ this as a principle in business, you would be in line with God's economy and He would therefore be obligated to prove Himself in this are. So then:

> A Financial Board should have ten (10) members.

> When sowing in business you should sow in tens - $10,000 or $10,000,000

And take note – watch the ten (10) nations, the ten nations that will control all the wealth of the world and business/trade. There is significance there!

God wants His people to trade in order to get interest for the Kingdom. He is always working and promoting those who are receiving interest! God does not deal with loss, He deals with interest and multiplication. He always wants us, according to Genesis 1: 28, to be fruitful and multiply and to fill the earth and also to have dominion over all living things; and no fruit or multiplication can come without a seed! There is a difference when we plant to receive interest!

Faithfulness

Faithfulness is a key ingredient in multiplication and fruitfulness as you trade, and it is a Biblical Principle. Being faithful brings greater authority, expansion and increase!

The reason many companies and individuals are experiencing loss is that they are not abiding by Biblical Principles. Faithfulness to the tasks and abiding by the Principles of God are what bring continued success in any endeavor!

Now according to the Scripture in Luke 19: 11 – 27, any person or organization that refuses your reign over them is an enemy. Look at Isaiah 60: 12 which specifically speaks of the result of those nations who refuse to serve those who are set over them. It says:

"For the nation and kingdom which will not serve you shall perish and those nations shall be utterly ruined."

You must understand that if God has placed you in a position of authority, the refusal of those over whom you are placed to accept you as such is rebellion and automatically makes them an enemy.

In verse 26, the conclusion of this Parable of Minas, makes two (2) points:

> The rule of God demands fearlessness and risk-taking

> Business is a risk, but with God it will bring interest.

Loosing What You Need

Luke 19: 28 – 30, Matthew 21: 1 – 3 and Mark 11: 1 – 6 all let us know that when Jesus had a need for something, He would give instructions to His disciples to loose whatever He had need of and bring it to Him. For us today, what the Lord is saying is that when you are in need of something, He has given us the authority to instruct the angels to loose whatever you need to bring it to us!

Whatever you need for the Kingdom's use you must loose it! Jesus at that time needed a colt – a brand new colt to use for the purpose of ministry. That colt was a vehicle, so in other words, He needed a brand new vehicle to take Him to where He needed to be and for a specific purpose. Today, you may need a new vehicle or a new building!

Jesus would send His disciples to go and loose whatever He needed. All Jesus would do is to discern where the wealth was and send them. (Luke 10 & 19)

God wants His leaders to send people to go and loose the resources and bring them to the leaders who have use for them; and as Jesus instructed, if anyone asked they were to say **"the Lord's house has need of it."**

In Genesis 24 Abraham sent out his servant to find a wife for His son. Both Abraham and his in-laws were blessed at the end of the day!

For a triumphal entry to take place there needs to be resources to take you there. Part of Jesus' success at that time was the Power of God working through Him, His humility/meekness, wisdom and unconditional love! But please note that meekness is not weakness!

Biblical Economics Wisdom

As you read Luke 20: 9, you will see that the Lease Option method used in Real Estate today was employed in this chapter.

Luke 20: 35 – 38 says:

"But those who are counted worthy to attain that age, and the resurrection from the dead, neither marry nor are given in marriage; nor can they die anymore, for they are equal to the angels and are sons of God being sons of the resurrection. But even Moses showed in the burning bush passage that the dead are raised, when he called the Lord, 'the God of Abraham, the God of Isaac, and the God of Jacob.' For He is not the God of the dead but of the living, for all live to Him."

God wants us to know that He is not the God of the dead but the God of the living, for all lives in Him! There was greater support for Jesus' ministry from Tax Collectors and sinners than from the *'just'* person! He nevertheless rules over nations.   Psalm 22: 28 shows that the Kingdom is the Lord's and He rules over nations and it is further expounded in Matthew 6: 13.

If you accept and understand this nugget, then you have received a level of wisdom that can take us to greater heights in God.

Prayer To Loose What You Need

Father, in the name of Jesus, I come to You now and I remind You that Your word says in Matthew 16: 19 that what we bind on earth is bound in heaven and what we loose on earth is loosed in heaven. Also, in Luke 19: 30 – 34 it states that Jesus commanded His disciples to go and loose the colt and bring it to Him for His use.

Therefore Father, in the name of Jesus, as I stand on your word, I send angels to loose brand new vehicles, aeroplanes, businesses, houses, buildings and money to us now! I send the angels to loose documents that will enhance the kingdom. Send to us people, millionaires, Tax Collectors and all resources necessary; release to us also good health, spiritual and natural children, protection of our riches and wealth, access to Radio and TV Stations and the anointing for wealth and miracles.

I thank you for it now in the name of Jesus! Amen!

Chapter 10

THE HOLY SPIRIT IN BUSINESS AND NATIONS

John 15: 26 – 27

By reading this Scripture you will understand that all your business ideas, your creative methods, increased sales, expansion of your organization come from the Holy Spirit!

As you carry out restructuring in our operations – justifications to cut costs, save jobs and increase efficiency and effectiveness – it is the Holy Spirit at work in you, and He gives you the know-how – the wisdom. Many persons will believe it is their intellect or brilliance. They think to themselves – *'I'm the best and it's a great marketing strategy. That's why it works.'* No! It is the Holy Spirit that empowers the person to come forth with that discovery or invention. It does not matter what religion you embrace – whether saved or not – the Holy Spirit is the leader, the teacher, the manager in business.

The Helper In Business

Now look at the word *'Helper'*. The word signifies *'an Intercessor'*. He will intercede for you when trouble is coming against you, your business and your family (as we are all related) for your growth and sound development. A divided family will result in a bankrupt business. Additionally, a wrecked family will eventually bring great loss to you and your company which results in your making wrong business decisions. So by making intercession for you, He ensures that you will be protected from danger.

The Comforter In Business

The term *'Comforter'* is an interesting one. Just think of yourself in a cold environment alone, a very cold place, and you need something to cover you from the cold – a blanket to keep you warm and to make you feel safe. This is what the Holy Spirit will do; He will keep you warm and protected; He will place a hedge around you and keep you from un-Godly elements that would affect you Even in difficult circumstances He will comfort you to survive it and pull through – even when business deals go sour; He will not allow us to make crazy decisions.

The Counselor In Business

The Holy Spirit will act as our Chief Lawyer. He will be a defense to us in legal matters and when critical business decisions are to be made. He will put words in our mouth during trials, negotiations, business deals, and wisdom to win our cases to defeat the enemy. He is our Chief Justice, Defender and Attorney who appears in court on our behalf, spiritually and naturally, teaches us the truth, in whatever deals there are and gives us general help, guidance, strength to endure hostility from other competitors and so on. It is the Holy Spirit that speaks to you in that little voice that many tend to say, *'something is telling me to do X'*, or *'something tells me I shouldn't do that'*.

Advocate

Planning strategies, business, market competition the fair way – once it is holy advice and not evil, it is the Holy Spirit.

Now there are nine (9) spiritual gifts that the Holy Spirit gives to the Body of Christ the believers to use to edify and to give glory to God. These gifts must also be used in business, for example, to hire good staff for:

> ➤ Better Sales

> ➤ Greater Output

> ➤ Increased Profit

Once you employ staff with these gifts, and give them the opportunity to use it in order to guide your company – not to sell or prostitute these gifts – then you would have made a great investment for your organization. This is particularly so in:

> ➤ Security Firms

> ➤ The Military

> ➤ The Police Force

and other such organizations that need Prophetic insight to discern market situations, fraud and leaking of company information. Such companies will also need the Prophetic insight to know:

> How to invest

> When to invest

> Where to invest

> What to invest

> Term of investment (whether short term or long term)

You would need the gift. It would also reduce your security cost and stamp out terrorists, because this gift would show you danger ahead. This is the gift America needs to get back as the real super-power, because it could be a tool used to advise Presidents on what tactics to employ regarding national level business, security, welfare, disaster preparedness and what measures to put in place for disasters; there is need for those gifts.

Any nation or business that refuses to allow the Holy Spirit, Who is also the Restrainer, to be a part of, or lead reforms and make decisions in the nation or in business will suffer great loss; not only businesses, but lives will be lost also. The Holy Spirit needs to be that COO for your nation, business, security decision and war plans. Once He is involved, less lives will be lost in any military conflict, because the king, President or Prime Minister would know exactly what strategies to implement, or which weapons to use, if any, to defeat the enemy. (II Kings 6: 17 esp. verses 10 – 12)

Now if the gifts of the Holy Spirit were in operation, many organizations' forecasts, budgets, strategies, and plans would be of such that those companies would not make a loss. This would be so, because the organization's decision-makers would know what to factor into that budget to prevent massive losses. They would also know what critical factors to focus on in order to prevent disasters.

It is the Holy Spirit Who empowered the prophets of old to give advice to kings about what to do during famine as in II Kings 6: 24 – 33 and II Kings 7.

Additionally, looking at Joseph, Daniel, Nehemiah and many others like them who advised kings, they were great leaders in their own right, and it was the Holy Spirit Who gave them wisdom. Even when Jesus was on earth – Luke 4: 18 – 19; Luke 2: 51 – 52, it was the Holy Spirit.

Further to this, it was also the Holy Spirit Who empowered Solomon with such wisdom, knowledge and understanding. He was a wise trader; many travelers from various parts of the world came to be instructed by the wisdom of the Holy Spirit through him. He had many vineyards and he knew business. He did not ask God for riches, he asked for wisdom, knowledge and understanding. These are gifts of the Holy Spirit, which you too can receive by seeking the things of God first. Matthew 6:33 declares that all things will be added to you; once you fully understand the role of the Holy Spirit in your life, business and nation, then there will be great wealth and prosperity.

Now there are many spirits, but one Holy Spirit Who is God! There are many symbols which represent Him:

➤ Fire (Acts 2: 3 – 4)

➤ A Dove (John 1: 32)

➤ Wind (Acts 2: 1- 2)

➤ Water (John 7: 37 – 39)

➤ Oil

➤ Seal (Ephesians 1:13; II Timothy 2: 19)

Word Of Wisdom

This is a supernatural gift given to accomplishing God's will in a given situation. For example, you may face a problem with a customer and it needs this supernatural wisdom to save the image and integrity of the company, *and* ensure that your customers or clients are left happy with whatever decisions are made. You must also ensure that you communicate to them, without this gift there will be serious loss.

It also gives you divine wisdom for quick problem-solving and a sense of divine direction. Wisdom works with knowledge and discernment.

Word Of Knowledge

This is a supernatural revelation of God's divine will and plans; and in the case of business, regarding:

➤ Enemy

> ➤ Friend

> ➤ Competitor

Additionally, it is supernatural insight or understanding of circumstances or a body of facts by revelation – which means it is without the assistance of human resources. It is moral wisdom for right living and relationship. This gift helps you to understand how the things of God relate to the natural things of the world. It will also help you better understand your staff and their motives.

Gift Of Faith

This is the supernatural belief in God without doubt. It is the key ingredient to:

> ➤ Combat unbelief

> ➤ Achieve things quickly that seem impossible to others

> ➤ Deal with adverse circumstances with trust in God

> ➤ Bring business visions to reality

> ➤ Believe all things are possible

Gift Of Healing

This is the supernatural healing without human aid. This gift can be used to help staff members that are sick to be able to function effectively on the job. It can also be used to help customers who might be sick, oppressed, depressed or demon-possessed. This gift will allow your customer or staff to cut down on the cost of medication and deliver them from bondage. By doing so you will have a healthier work force, better customer service, which will allow your staff and customers to cut down on their health bills and invest that money into your organization. Staff will also reduce the amount spent yearly on insurance coverage. Through this gift, God will reveal ways and things to use to bring healing to someone.

Working Of Miracles

This is supernatural power to intervene and counteract earthly and evil forces. By doing so you will have better business deals and prosperity, you will use this gift when circumstances are working against you. It also brings authority over sin, Satan, sickness and the binding forces of this age.

Now you must understand that evil forces are real against businesses. People will also curse or speak negative things against your business. This gift – the Working Of Miracles – will also help you out of bankruptcy. When there is no way out, this gift will create creative miracles in a situation.

Prophecy

This is divinely inspired and anointed utterance manifestation of the Spirit of God – not intellect (I Corinthians 12: 7)

This gift will help your company to move forward, it will also guide you as to:

> What action you must take to move forward.

> What God will do in a period to come if you will obey Him.

This gift is the best to guide you because it is directed by the Holy Spirit. It will:

> Encourage you in a difficult situation for edification and wisdom

> Inform you as to the strategies you can prepare. (Interestingly, you can even prepare your budget through the gift of prophecy.)

> It will also reveal who you are in God and things to come for your life.

All businesses need this gift of prophecy for guidance and so on.

Discerning Of Spirits

Supernatural power to detect the realm of the spirits and their activities, this gift will protect you from:

> ➢ Fraudulent business deals

> ➢ Wrong Motives

and tells you:

> ➢ How to deal with your clients or business partners

> ➢ How to function in order to build trust

> ➢ How to employ staff

Once this gift is in operation you cannot be easily fooled. Without this gift you will be carried away by the wiles and trickery of men.

It gives you supernatural revelation of plans and purposes of the enemy and His forces and by what measure. This gift also helps you to identify safeguards you need to put in place to prevent losses. Many times people also tend to say something like, *'I don't trust that person!'* That is the gift operating in you, and by ignoring that warning, you let your guard down only to be tricked. Learn to recognize the gift that is in you for with this gift you will also discern market conditions.

This gift along with the other two (2) previously discussed can help you to truly experience success and victory.

Diverse Tongues

This is a gift needed in this era for all to move forward. As long as you embrace these gifts, then you will be on the right path for prosperity, you will not lose what you already recovered. It is to protect you from the enemy. It is your Spiritual degree to take you not only to the top, but to give you power, wisdom and revelation of the mysteries of things according to Isaiah 45, as well as the revelation of hidden treasures.

Worship Music In Business

You must understand that all that has been created, was made to serve and worship God – everything under the sun, according to Psalm 148, 149 and 150 (esp. verse 6).

"Let everything that has breath praise the Lord. Praise the Lord!"

Now the devil deeply desires to be worshipped because he knows the value and the power of worship. Satan was the cherub that had fallen and even now, he still desires to be worshipped, so he will orchestrate various activities and situations so that worship is directed to him rather than to the true and living God. When you praise God, the presence of His spirit is in your midst – in the business – and the presence of the Lord is ushered into our midst and into our business through worship music. Another way to usher in the presence of the Lord is to have worship in the morning to give God thanks for each day. These benefits would accrue:

➢ Increased Sales

➢ New customers to the organization

➢ Greater Profit

➢ New Revelation

➢ Victory in a difficult task

Once you refuse to have the presence of the Lord at your place of business, there will be doom and problems and darkness will be over your business. There will be no growth, crime and violence will take over until your business closes.

Worship is what brings light! Begin to create that environment with worship music and watch what the Lord will do. It is a blessing that you don't have to pay for – it is free. Where the presence of the Lord is there is liberty. It also brings healing to your business.

Chapter 11

PROPHECIES TO BUSINESS PERSONS

1. God is calling on the rich creditors and leaders to restore to those they have robbed with high interest rates, and those whose assets they have taken away; so that they and their companies will live. (Ezekiel 18: 7 – 9)

2. Failure to follow God's instruction to restore what was robbed will bring Bankruptcy, loss and ruin (Ezekiel 18: 12 – 13) to you individually and to your organization. Stop the usury! Failure to do so will result in disaster!

3. In the 7th year as in Deuteronomy 15: 1 – 6 there must be debt write-offs and it will bring great blessing to your company:

    ➢   Expansion of Business

    ➢   Takeover of other Businesses by your Business

    ➢   Going into other nations

    ➢   Increased Asset Base

    ➢   Increase in Profit

    ➢   New Product Ideas

➤ Stability and growth even during famine and recession

If businesses and leaders want to survive, they must restore those things they have changed, such as high interest rate; (Nehemiah 5: 1 – 11) that salvation will come into their house. (Luke 19: 1 – 10) They will receive these benefits:

➤ Deliverance

➤ Soundness

➤ Prosperity

➤ Happiness

➤ Preservation

➤ Rescue

According to Exodus 22: 25 – 27, God is calling on the lenders/creditors to stop this high interest rate that is putting His people in bondage!

According to Psalm 15: 5, stop the usury and be blessed. Leviticus 25: 35 – 37.

God is calling His people to sow their way out of debt and be debt-free! (Genesis 8: 22; Genesis 26)

Seek God first when you are in debt. (Jeremiah 33: 3) Seek the prophet to help you out of debt. (II Kings 4: 1 – 7)

If, for example, you desire a debt free house, sow one month's mortgage. If you desire a debt-free car, sow the equivalent of a month's payment and watch God pay off your debts.

Obey the voice of God according to Deuteronomy 28, and come out of debt. Obedience is the number one (1) key to coming out of debt.

Deuteronomy 24: 6 declares that you must not take away the only asset(s) they had to use as collateral for a loan. If they are unable to make payments on time, taking away their only method for acquiring their daily bread is not going to make it any better!

There are two (2) things you must remember:

➢ Unforgiveness will keep you in debt (Matthew 6: 12)

➢ Fear and doubt will sink you into debt. (Matthew 14) Keep your eyes on Jesus, not on the debt!

God wants laws put in place to protect the poor from high interest loans and unfair business practices. The Government should put in place Period Loans, not Commercial Loans with lower interest during times of hardship, so that they can survive and come out of debt.

Chapter 12

ALL THE WEALTH BELONGS TO GOD

There are several Scriptures that declare the simple fact that all the wealth belongs to God. Once every New Millionaire understands what this entails, he or she is on his or her way to true wealth.

I Chronicles 29 (especially 10 – 16)

Psalm 8: 4 – 8

Psalm 50: 9 – 11

Haggai 1: 1 – 11 (especially 6 – 8)

Malachi 3

Deuteronomy 8: 17 – 18

Every government and every individual should be concerned about the natural resources of the earth and other spheres of life that inhabit it. The dominion given to man over the earth makes us as human beings, accountable for it.

You must always consider our ways when you seek to use the Lord's money, for your purpose, and neglect His house and His ministries that seek to accomplish His mission.

There is no excuse that can be given by individuals, nations and businesses for not giving to build the house of the Lord, when all the blessing, wealth and resources are given to them by the Lord according to Deuteronomy 8: 18. It states that God is the one who gives power to get wealth. *'Power'* means *'strength, vigor, force, or capacity'*. *'Wealth'* means *'substance, capacity or ability whether physically or spiritually'*.

Success and talent are given by God. Moses warned in Deuteronomy 8: 17 that you should never say in your heart, your power and the might of your hand have gained you this wealth. All the wisdom, increase, favor, promotion are given by God. When you make a profit, it is given by God, and every increase you receive God must get His portion. The Tithes is for God and the firstfruit is for God. You must attend three (3) times per year before God with your gift the three (3) feasts. If there was any debate or disobedience then such persons and their vision would be short-lived. Likewise, your disobedience in this area today will cause you, your organization and your nation to be short-lived. God clearly speaks in Haggai 2: 6 – 8 – that He will shake nations. He speaks that the silver is His and the gold is His also.

Haggai 1: 10 – 11 state that God controls the economy of a nation. Once man is not in compliance with God and He is not getting His portion, as the Chief investor, who makes everything possible then He will call a drought, famine, serious recession, as well as natural and economic disasters. You will also experience no growth. Every area will be seriously affected.

The only areas that will find growth are those in compliance with God's instructions. This is the seriousness of God's calling for His money that is owed to Him, not just that, but financial institutions and individuals will have to add their one-fifth (1/5), according to Leviticus 27: 31

If you read Genesis 41: 34, you will see that Joseph instructed Pharaoh to collect the fifth part of the land of Egypt in the year of plenty.

Now understand that the term *'produce'* means *'manufactured goods, raw materials, fruit, harvest, agricultural and natural produce, profit or monetary value.'*

As you read the Scripture you will realize that Egypt was not paying Tithes, nor were they giving First-fruits and sowing seed to the true and living God. They were, instead, paying homage to false gods; like the fertility god, whom they thought to be responsible for their wealth. Many millionaires and wealthy businesses are channeling their money or giving to the wrong source, without realizing that God must get His portion.

In the book of Malachi 3, God states He will be a swift witness against all those who affect the Economy:

➢ Sorcerers

➢ Adulterers

➢ Perjurers

➢ Exploiters

Now, In Malachi 3: 5, God specifically stated that He would be against nations that exploit wage earners, widows and orphans, and against those who turn away an alien. As you read this, you will see similarities with the way immigration systems within nations operate. How a nation deals with immigrants will affect the nation and bring judgement on the economy.

How many may look at Malachi 3: 8 – 10, God clearly addresses nations and individuals regarding robbing God. Theft is a crime in any realm – natural or spiritual. When a person carries out robbery, if they are found guilty, they will be sentenced by natural laws. It is highly hypocritical when individuals and nations seek to maintain these natural laws, yet they are carrying out criminal acts of robbery against God when they neglect or refuse to give their Tithes and Offerings. They don't realize that the same principle applies when dealing with the things of God. They don't realize that things are taking place within the Heavenly Court and sentencing takes place both on individuals and on nations concerning issues such as:

➤   Crime

➤   Famine

➤   Poor Economic Conditions

➤   Injustice

➤   Curses

➤   Plagues

➢ No Growth

Remember that God is the one who gives the blessings in the first place, so giving back to Him should be a pleasure!

When you fail to pay taxes to your tax institution, there is a penalty for late payments and legal matters to recover. That is the same principle that Malachi 3: 6 speaks of, and God does not change in this respect. Malachi 3: 10 clearly outlines that *"... all Tithes must be brought into the storehouse..."*, and the local church is the storehouse. This so that *"... there may be food in My house, and try Me now in this."* Therefore:

➢ God's Pastors will be paid good salaries

➢ Souls will be won

➢ His business on earth will be taken care of

➢ The poor will be fed

Any attempt made by world leaders by way of laws put in place to stop God's instructions regarding His money coming in through the nations, must be able to deal with the curses/judgement on the economy.

Additionally, anyone who tries to put laws in place to dry up the Tithes of the people will and must be ready to face the wrath of the true and living God. Nations will crumble.

Individuals and nations must recognize that those who fight against the prosperity of the Church will also encounter the wrath of God because all belong to God.

God is now building His kingdom not for man, but for Himself. The kingdom belongs to God! I Chronicles 29 lets us know that and gives us pointers to follow.

> ➤ I Chronicles 29: 2 shows you that God wants His people to prepare, with all their might, the things (including money) necessary to build God's House.

> ➤ I Chronicles 29: 3 encourages you to set your affections on building God's House. When you do so, you will give more than enough.

> ➤ I Chronicles 29: 5 reveals that all those who are going to build God's House must consecrate themselves holy to the Lord.

> ➤ I Chronicles 29: 6 – 7 reveal that leaders must be the first to be willing to give to build the Lord's House.

> ➤ I Chronicles 29: 9 reveals that people must have a loyal heart and they must offer willingly to build.

God always tests the hearts of leaders first to see if they will give willingly, according to I Chronicles 29: 17. The same spirit at the top of the hierarchy is the same spirit that will be found at the bottom. Pray that the people will have a loyal heart to give.

The categories that supported Solomon's Ministry according to II Chronicles 9: 14 were:

> ➤ Travelling Merchants

> ➤ Traders

God is paying close attention to these categories of workers because He is ready to bless if they bless His house. In fact, Proverbs 8: 13 – 21 speak of the blessings given by God to those who love Him and the wealth to be inherited by them.

Additionally, no attempt must be made to tax God's ministers as in Matthew 17: 24 – 27, they are sons. The kings and leaders of the earth do not tax their sons, only strangers. You are among the sons, and Jesus claimed exemptions from tax as the son of God who is King of the universe. The only reason Jesus paid was that He would not be branded as profane and irreligious.

The Power To Get Wealth - Deuteronomy 8

God gives us the power to get wealth. Now many businesses are blaming banks for what is happening. Now if the banks are always successfully making millions, why are they blamed when they fail? Why not look at the bigger picture? Business is a chain reaction. Now God is letting us know that He is in control of all business transactions. It does not matter how bright mankind is, without God businesses will come to nothing! Banks were structured to make millions from the application of High Interest Rates. But what were the banks doing with the large profits:

- ➤ Did God get His portion?

- ➤ Did the poor benefit?

- ➤ Did they use the profits to sponsor evil things that offend God?

- ➤ When they were enjoying the benefits, did God get the glory?

In addition to this:

- ➤ How much assets have they taken away from the poor and sold to their friends as was done in Nehemiah 5?

- ➤ Have you taken note of the Scripture in Habakkuk 2: 5 – 11 which speaks about plundering?

- ➤ What did the Scripture say in Job 27?

- ➤ Do business people think God's word will fall to the ground?

- ➤ What about Seedtime and harvest according to Genesis 8: 22?

Many will say they give to the poor but if you give to the poor you give to the Lord. You may give to the poor, but you refuse to give God His Tithes and offering according to Malachi 3: 10. Hence they will no longer benefit from the seven (7) blessings from above.

Fair Business Practice

God wants businesses to know that God is in charge of their success, not them. It will not be business as usual anymore. The economists will not be able to predict this famine; not until they get back to basics and look at the foundation of prosperity.

Neither businessmen nor political leaders will be successful unless they seek God's servants for advice.

> ➢ Do the banks give debt cancellation so that they can receive a blessing – according to Deuteronomy 15, Matthew 6: 12 and Matthew 18: 21 – 35.

> ➢ On what principles were the banks and other businesses operating? On man's or God's? Unless you return to Biblical Principles, then more banks and businesses will shut down.

Psalm 10: 4 says:

"The wicked in his proud countenance does not seek God; God is in none of his thoughts."

The secularization of any nations, with its removal of any move of God in their schools, businesses or politics is a step toward its ultimate downfall and judgement.

If you deny Christ on earth before men, the same will happen to you. Matthew 10: 32; Luke 12: 8 -9 including your business.

Chapter 13

KEYS TO WEALTH

Some people will want to seek your Godly counsel, but not want to be seen with you in public. They are afraid of what their colleagues will say, according to John 3. They will come to you by night, just as Nicodemus did. Nicodemus knew that Jesus could not do these miracles unless God was with Him. Yet he only visited with Christ at night.

Sometimes when you see God bringing down an organization, through bankruptcy, for example, it is for our benefit and for the nation's as well. This is so because most of these organizations sponsored or supported evil activities with the profits they made. So you must rejoice when God closes down these organizations. Matthew 6: 10 says:

"Your kingdom come, Your will be done on earth as it is in heaven."

As long as their businesses are not establishing God's kingdom on earth, and has instead been establishing Satan's kingdom, it must be closed down, according to Revelation 18. Only those that are establishing God kingdom will stand.

Matthew 6: 12 state, that God's people must pray each day for debt write-offs; and as it is done to you, you must do it to others. In addition to that, forgiveness is not just about offence committed against you or that you commit against others; but the greatest unforgiveness is debt that could be forgiven and written off and not only by individuals or organizations. Unforgiveness of debt will stop God from realizing a blessing on an individual, organization or nation. Remember that debt is bondage. God does not want His people to be in bondage. He wants them to freely serve Him. That is why Deuteronomy 15: 1 – 11 show what a creditor should do to get the blessing of the Lord. Verse 6 especially shows how God would establish him in the nations. Additionally, He speaks about the poor, within our gates, legal place, city or community.

Leaders must cut back during recession. The first thing you must cut is expenses – according to Nehemiah 5: 18 – because the bondage is heavy. In this Scripture, Nehemiah led by example.

Understand this:

1   God wants businessmen and nations to understand that they need to extend the mercy and compassion that they want God to extend to them. It is the same God that wants you to extend to others, Matthew 18: 23 – 27.

2   God wants His people not to be like the unforgiving servants. Once there is forgiveness of debts, you must do the same with someone else. (Matthew 18: 28 – 31).

3   God wants all to know that He is the Chief Creditor, hence, you must ensure that you never

allow yourselves to be called wicked servants. Forgive someone today of their debt to you (vs. 32). When someone is in debt, and has nothing to repay, forgive him/her of his/her debt according to Luke 7: 40 – 41. Write off the debt!

In order to stay ahead during the famine and recession:

➢ Businessmen and Leaders must start to lead by example, by taking a salary cut and reducing other expenses during hard times. Do not ask the poor to make sacrifices; the oppressor must be dealt with to rescue the poor.

➢ The usury must stop! Businessmen, Political Leaders must walk in the fear of God. (Nehemiah 5: 9 – 10)

➢ God wants leaders to restore to the people their assets that are being taken away in recession/famine. (Nehemiah 5: 11 – 12)

➢ Failure to restore to the poor will result in further famine and retribution. It will become worse until the leaders bow! Selling these assets to their friends at 'below market' value will not work this time.

➢ According to Nehemiah 5: 15, God is going to deal with leaders who lay burdens on the people and those who do not fear God!

You are placing an entire generation in debt; there is no freedom from slavery until you are debt-free. Christ redeemed us from bondage! It is Satan's wicked schemes that put us back into bondage – in debt – to control us in order to afflict and destroy us. They have taken away the vineyards and land – the inheritance – from the people. They have had to mortgage their home and property in order to buy food, and to deal with the famine and recession – all this to survive!

According to Nehemiah 5: 1 – 13, it is clear that there are several things needed for financial survival during a famine.

> ➤ During a famine or economic crisis, there should be tax breaks given. By so doing, it will help to bring people out of debt and prevent them from getting into further financial bondage. There should be no taxes levied. Additionally, recognize that during recession, paying taxes will bring families into insolvency.

> ➤ There needs to be an audit done in order to deal with organizations that oppress the poor during recession.

> ➤ God is calling on leaders to lead by example as Nehemiah did; self-sacrifice is necessary for leadership.

Authority For Wealth

Now, Jesus could get anything He needed in Ministry. When He needed a place to celebrate the Passover with His disciples, He just sent out two (2) of His disciples as

He did in Mark 11: 1 – 6 or Matthew 21: 1 – 3. He just sent them to say the Teacher said 'where is the guest room in which I may celebrate the Passover with my disciples.

Mark 14: 15 states that He will then show you one large Upper Room furnished and prepared, and there make ready for you. This shows that Jesus has people who would sow into His ministry, every time He needed He asked. By obeying the Master, apostles or other servants by giving them the necessary things they need to carry out their ministry you will be greatly blessed. This is also proven in Luke 5. You will make a large catch! Fish is symbolic of souls, finances for you and your business partners – the New Millionaire will obey and be blessed!

Jesus always used unusual signs as a cue to bless His people. A man carrying a pitcher of water was an unusual sight in a society where women always did that kind of work.

In Psalm 50: 10 – 11 it is clearly stated that the cattle on a thousand hills belongs to the Lord. The number **'1000'** means **'the beginning of maturity.'**

As millionaires you have the authority to petition to God to sell the cattle and give you the money or to give you the cattle to invest. You have this access, but God wants you to think big! Don't think poverty, think WEALTH, think RICH; ask the Lord to release the wealth!

Verse 12 tells you that the entire world belongs to God, and all His fullness within. All God wants us to do is to obey Him and be blessed as He stated in Exodus 19: 5 – 6:

➤   Obey His voice

➤   Keep His Covenant

Then *"you shall be a special treasure to Me above all people for all the earth is Mine"* (for God)

Further blessings in verse 6 you shall be to Him a kingdom of priests and a holy nation. These are the words which you shall speak to the Children of Israel.

The Lord clearly outlined in His Scripture what you should do to be that, or be in the category of special treasure, not an ordinary person, but to be that New Millionaire by abiding by His principles.

In Psalm 50: 13 – 15 God wants us to come up and give Him thanksgiving! By paying our Tithes according to Malachi 3: 10

Pay your vows to Him, sow seed according to Genesis 8: 22, then call upon Him in the day of trouble and He will deliver you, and you will glorify Him.

Prosperity – III John Verse 2

There are different levels of prosperity. By reading this Scripture, realize that God wants you to be balanced in all areas:

> ➢ Spirituality

> ➢ Physically

> ➢ Emotionally

> ➢ Materially

Now many prosper materially, but not spiritually! If they are not balanced then those persons will walk right into bankruptcy. The key thing is to first be balanced spiritually, according to Matthew 6: 33. Then all things will be added to you. Your soul must prosper! Don't seek wealth unless you are going to continue to seek God that your soul prospers.

God has raised up many millionaires in the past who prosper in material things. The mistake they made is that they ceased to prosper in their souls. They stopped seeking the Kingdom. They started to focus more on their material wealth. Hence other areas started to deteriorate, for example.

> ➢ Health (physically, spiritually and emotionally)

> ➢ Relationships

With all the cash they had there was no peace!

You are seeing many dying and they leave their wealth for charity or the state. It was too late when they decided

to deal with their souls! If they were living Matthew 6:
33, the Kingdom of God would give them long life! No
sickness or disease would have afflicted them. Do not
look on prosperity with single sight!

The New Millionaire must not make the mistake of those
in the past, he/she must be wiser – God is your first
source!

Chapter 14

WISDOM THROUGH MISTAKES TO BRING SOLUTIONS

Throughout life mistakes are made, but the New Millionaire must recognize that through mistakes he/she gains wisdom having learned from the mistakes, and then grasp the opportunity to develop solutions. Remember:

➤ Wisdom comes through mistakes

➤ Never make decisions based on emotions. Separate emotional issues from decision-making, and make decisions by the leading of the Holy Spirit

➤ One wrong decision will lead you into financial bondage in addition to other kinds of trouble

➤ The general aim in business is to make profit – honest profit – and not a loss. According to Matthew 25: 14 – 30, God always demands increase (See also Luke 19: 11 – 26)

➤ According to Luke 19: 27, only those who decide to invest whatever the Lord gives them for the kingdom purpose is considered a friend of God! Those who refuse to invest in the kingdom can consider themselves an enemy, because they refuse the reign of the Lord over them.

➢ Investors who refuse to have the Lord reign over them by following his instructions and principles with regard to giving to the Kingdom, will have their favor taken away. (Luke 19: 26; Luke 8: 18)

➢ Trading is done in order to make a profit or to achieve double on what God has given to you. God desires investors from whom He can get His portion, as is found in Luke 19: 23, whether it be money, gifts, talents or souls!

➢ Luke 8: 14 tells us that those who hear God's words and allow them to fall among thorns when they hear them go out and are choked with the cares of the world, riches and pleasures of life and bring no fruit to maturity, God will judge. (See also Luke 8: 18)

➢ Luke 19: 11 – God always gives double blessings to those who trade in His business so that He can get a profit. He doubles their territory because of their faithfulness, and He doubles their authority.

➢ There is a transfer of blessings/wealth and authority in the Kingdom, because of faithfulness and hard work, as well as how you trade the talents that the Lord has given you.

➢ Those who bury or refuse to impart what God has given them will be evaluated by God, according to Luke 19: 20, and if they have not increased, particularly in the area of souls, will be in trouble.

> ➤ God is now carrying out evaluations in the Body of Christ, the secular entities, even in politics with regard to what He gave each to trade to see if He will be collecting any 'interest'.

> ➤ Those whom the Lord has given Spiritual gifts and talents and are not using it to God's glory – by way of interest in souls – will have their authority transferred to someone else. (See Luke 19: 26; Luke 8: 18)

> ➤ When God has given authority to transact His business, He expects faithfulness so that He can earn interest.

Ezra 3: 5 – 7 tells us that the people gave money to build the Temple:

> ➤ Meat

> ➤ Drink

> ➤ Oil

Therefore:

Always think like the rich/wealthy – be business-like, seek ways to make profit not loss. Everything must make good business sense.

If you do not think and operate in a business-like fashion, you will end up in poverty – regardless of who you transact with. The New Millionaire business people must not compromise business practices – not even with their friends. They must establish the principles.

The spiritual man will show compassion in business. The natural man does not show compassion in business. You must recognize that there needs to be a balance in business if there is going to be long term success.

Our thinking must be like a Godly businessman. You must do things from the point of view of, *'what would God do in this situation?'* That is the way of thinking that you must adapt. You cannot be successful unless you read and apply the word of God.

A Godly businessman thinks as the Scripture says in Philippians 4: 8. This Scripture gives us 8 principles to be successful. It says you ought to think on/embrace things that are:

- ➢ True

- ➢ Honest

- ➢ Just

- ➢ Pure

- ➢ Lovely

- ➢ Good

- ➢ Virtuous

The Rich Godly Businessmen must:

Think as Philippians 4: 13 – *"I can do all things through Christ who strengthens me."*

➢   Know how to <u>be</u> in all things – Philippians 4: 11 – 12

➢   Know that God will supply all your needs according to His riches in glory by Christ Jesus.

➢   Follow this Scripture – Philippians 4: 6 – and apply Prayer, Supplication and Thanksgiving to your daily lifestyle.

➢   Learn to catch fish, not get handouts at all times. You must learn how to establish businesses.

Always remember:

➢   Time is valuable. Your time costs something. If someone wants to spend time with you, to get your wisdom, they have to compensate you – particularly if that is your business. (II Chronicles 9: 23 – 24)

➢   Money is of greater value to you only when you have God. Having money without God is unwise and will lead to destruction. (See Luke 12: 13 – 21)

> The rich Godly men must study money and wealth if they want to keep it. The first place to study is the **Holy Bible**. They also need to read books on money, attend related seminars, and visit clubs that deal with money.

When you make mistakes financially, use your mistake as a path to the future. Use your mistake as a platform to your wealth. Always remember that your mistake costs you something. Use the lessons learned from your mistakes to recover your costs in the future. For example, from the mistakes you have made in your past, what have you learnt? Have you identified the Do's and Don'ts? Use that information to:

> Hold Seminars

> Write a book

> Offer Consultancy services

> Solve Problems for others

> Increase your wisdom – if so, what are you going to do with that wisdom?

Use your mistakes to recover more than what you have lost. Wisdom comes through pain. Someone has to pay for that pain. There is a price for the anointing; it never comes free.

If there is a value for the anointing, then others will respect it and pay for it or sow into your anointing. Even

161

regarding salvation, Jesus Christ paid for it so that you may receive life! (See II Chronicles 9: 22 – 25)

The rich Godly man has to think big; they have think of being richer than the world or the unsaved man; according to II Chronicles 9: 22, God wants him to be richer.

Keys To Success

Here are several keys to success of which you must take keen note.

> ➢ Always remember that you cannot move to the next level, unless someone promotes you spiritually or naturally.

> ➢ You cannot be promoted unless you follow instruction.

> ➢ Remember that whatever you do when you are in the seat of authority will be done back to you as you exit. For example, if you succeed through rebellion or any other un-Godly manner, it will be done to you in return.

> ➢ Success only comes through living by the word. You cannot effectively preach or teach what you haven't walked.

➤ Always remember that blessings come from above not beneath.

➤ Create an image in your mind of where you want to see the vision or your dream in the next three (3) years.

➤ You cannot be successful unless you become a success in someone else's vision.

➤ Always remember, nothing is impossible with God.

➤ The environment you create determines what you attract. Therefore, fix up your environment, improve yourself, dress for the part you seek and be aware.

➤ Remember, there is no limit in God. Faith brings success and so does obedience. You must do what God says you are to do. Don't look at the dollar amount.

➤ Your blessings are wrapped up in the vision of which you are a part– not your personal vision.

➤ Everything in life is an exchange – nothing is truly free.

➤ Everything you do must have a market impact – hence strong tactics and strategies.

➤ Look at your surroundings and see if the decisions you are making are Kingdom-minded or selfish.

It is interesting to realize that there are many churches/ministries that have a great or even unusual anointing, but they need to attract those with the resources to help them get to the next level. The only way that can happen is to listen to the Lord and move when you see the resources begin to dry up. God is saying that you are to move to the next level or area.

Money, Wisdom And Vision

According to Ecclesiastes 10: 19, money answers all things. Habakkuk 2 speaks of the vision. In light of these two (2) Scriptures, there are several things you need to keep in mind.

> For every plan to be brought forth, there is a money value to it

> Money is what brings forth money

> To market your plan it takes money

> To finance your vision it takes money

> To increase your organization it takes money

> To live peacefully it takes money

> To bring you to a certain spiritual level it takes money

> To pay your bills and be debt free it takes money

> ➢ To be strife-free it takes money (Poverty brings strife)

> ➢ For wisdom to be heard it takes money (Ecclesiastes 9: 13 – 18)

> ➢ You can't win a battle without money

> ➢ Certain wisdom or knowledge can't be imparted to you without money   For example, you will need to attend seminars, schools and they cost money.

> ➢ To rise to power, with influence, you need money.

ALSO

> ➢ Money brings you before great men, because money attracts money

> ➢ Money gives you power

> ➢ Money also helps to get justice

> ➢ Money will cause your enemy to think twice before attacking you

> ➢ Money causes and ends wars

Proverbs 10: 15 says:

"The rich man's wealth is His strong city, the destruction of the poor is their poverty."

This tells us that poverty brings destruction.

➢   Money can bring in millions of souls for God

➢   Money feeds the poor, the fatherless and the widows and is part of prosperity with God.

➢   Money can either break you or make you. It brings you in great company and money takes you out of great company.

Ecclesiastes 6: 12 says declares:

"For wisdom is a defense as money is a defense, money will bring protection."

Ecclesiastes 6: 1 – 2 tell you:

"There is an evil which I have seen under the sun, and it is common among men: a man to whom God has given riches and wealth and honor, so that he lacks nothing for himself of all he desires…"

Wealth, riches and honor are powers given by God for you according to Luke 12: 20 – 21. God wants us to lay up treasures in heaven. Getting wealth is a power given by God. To enjoy wealth is a power given by God. Job 21: 10 says that God does not want us take His blessing for granted.

Ecclesiastes 10: 5 – 7 show that God wants His people who are rich to rise up from a lowly place.

The Scripture says:

There is an evil I have seen under the sun, as an error proceeding from the ruler. Folly is set in great dignity, while the rich sit in a lowly place. I have seen servants on horses, while princes walk on the ground like servants."

It is important to note that the term *'servants'* in this context refers to *'those who don't believe in God'*; and the term *'princes'* here refers to *'God's servants'*.

Chapter 15

8 KEYS OF WISDOM FOR THE GOVERNMENT TO REDUCE DEBT AND CRIME – WORLD LEADERS TAKE NOTE!

1. Restore Temple Worship - starting at the Head House in the nation. (II Chronicles 29: 20–36). Ask the people of the nation to bring a Sin Offering that the Priestly Order will be restored and that the blessing will return to the nation.

2. The Leaders of nations must call all the Five-fold Ministry personnel – (Ephesians 4: 11) for a day of Cleansing and Sanctification, especially for the resources of the land that was wasted and for the corruption. (II Chronicles 29: 3 – 19)

3. Keep the Three (3) Annual Feasts - according to Exodus 23: 14 – 17 and Numbers 28 & 29 held in April, June and September. The end of September to mid-October is the month of Tishri, and this is a month during which, a window is opened for the nation! The nation needs to utilize the season for change and healing in the nation. It is the end of an Agricultural Year and the beginning of another. A very special time for change based on the Jewish calendar. That is the period for calling the assembly. (Numbers 29: 12 – 39) October 1 and 8 are particularly special during this time. (Genesis 8: 5)

4. Call a 7-day Fast in October. It must be called by the Leader of the Nation so that the Lord can heal the people and the Land. (II Chronicles 30: 19 – 27).

> ➤ During this Fast, the nations' leaders must sow a seed of $8,000 – *'8'* means *'new beginning; new birth; new monarchy; circumcision'* (Genesis 8: 13; Genesis 17: 12; Exodus 22: 30), and *'Thousand'* means *'the beginning of maturity'* (II Chronicles 1).

> ➤ The remaining members of the Administration must sow a seed of $11,000 each. *'11'* means *'end, paradigm shift; divine injunction'* (Matthew 20: 9, 12) and it is the number used also when power changes hands. [Use holy men of God to break the curses, not religious men nor theologians]

5. Remove the carved images and tear down the high places and wooden images. Get rid of all the things that are embedded in our nation as culture which are witchcraft! (II Chronicles 34: 1 – 7)

6. There needs to be a holy Priest and a holy Prophet who are neutral and without personal motives to instruct the leader of the nation in the Word of the Lord, to make decisions, as major challenges are ahead for the Administration; especially today, with the corruption of past Administrations since

the time of Independence. (II Chronicles 34: 8 – 33). By doing so, judgement will escape the nation and reform will take place.

7. Reform cannot truly take place until the spiritual aspect is first dealt with. Failure, Crime and Debt will worsen and there will be numerous strikes, demonstration and riots. (Isaiah 17)

8. Reducing Debt and Crime can only be a reality if you apply Biblical Principles. It will be easy if you seek the right source. The answer is in the Word of God. Failure to execute God's desire for and upon the nation will only create for you a huge nightmare!

I Corinthians 2: 6 – 16 say:

*"However, we speak wisdom among those who are mature, yet not the wisdom of this age, nor the rulers of this age who are coming to nothing. But we speak the wisdom of God in a mystery, the hidden wisdom which God ordained before the ages for our glory, which none of the rulers of this age knew for had they known they would not have crucified the Lord of glory. But as it is written: 'Eye has not seen, nor has ear heard, nor have entered into the heart of man the things which God has prepared for those who love Him.' But God has revealed them to us through His Spirit. For the Spirit searches all things, yes, the deep things of God. For what man knows the things of a man except the spirit of the man which is in him? Even so no one knows the things of God except the Spirit of God. Now we have received, not the spirit of the world, but the Spirit who is from God that we might know the things that have been freely given to us by God. **These things we also speak, not in words which man's wisdom teaches but**

which the Holy Spirit teaches comparing spiritual things with spiritual. But the natural man does not receive the things of the Spirit of God, for they are foolishness to him; nor can he know them, because they are spiritually discerned. *But he who is spiritual judges all things yet he himself is rightly judged by no one. For who has known the mind of the Lord that he may instruct Him? But we have the mind of Christ."*

Chapter 16

THE NEW MILLIONAIRE

While the term is a new one, the concept of the New Millionaire is not new. In fact, there are several examples of the New Millionaire throughout the Bible – Joseph, Job, Daniel, Ruth and Esther. The New Millionaire is one who commits himself/herself to the Triune God (The Father, Jesus the Son and the Holy Spirit), lives by the principles of the Word of God and obeys the voice of the Lord to the point of action. Further to this, The New Millionaire is one who:

➤ Does not compromise concerning the things or instructions of God

➤ Acknowledges and fully accepts Jesus Christ as his/her Lord and Savior

➤ Believes in and embraces the power of the Holy Spirit

➤ Walks in the fear and favor of God

➤ Uses his/her wealth to help build the kingdom, fund God-given visions and support a Godly lifestyle

According to Psalm 25: 9, the New Millionaire must also be *__humble__*! There are benefits to being humble. You can receive:

> ➤ Guidance in justice

> ➤ Wisdom, Knowledge and Understanding

> ➤ Mercy and Truth

Undoubtedly, the concept of the New Millionaire is embedded in the Word of God.

The New Millionaire And The Word

Psalm 37: 23 -24 tell you that:

"The steps of a good man are ordered by the Lord, and He delights in his ways. Though he fall he shall not be utterly cast down, for the Lord upholds him with His hand."

Once you are righteous, God will order your steps! He will protect you and He will lead you into prosperity and green pastures.
Additionally, Proverbs 24: 16 says that the righteous may fall seven times and rise again, but the wicked shall fall by calamity. Falling is not fatal, except to the wicked.

Psalm 37: 25 – 26 state further, that God will not forsake the righteous, nor allow his descendants – Spiritual and Natural – to beg bread. Verse 26 says, *"He is ever merciful, and lends, and his descendants are blessed."* This lets you know that there is great blessing for your descendants.

God wants those who desire to be New Millionaires to pursue righteousness because there are great blessings in doing so. He wants the New Millionaire to know that with righteousness comes great blessing and that includes riches and wealth! He has a innumerable, immeasurable benefits to be released to the righteousness - and these benefits ill cause them to become the New Millionaire.

Benefits For Those Who Fear The Lord

> ➤ Guidance   – Him shall He teach the way He chooses (Psalm 25: 12)

> ➤ Spiritual Prosperity - He Himself shall dwell in prosperity (Psalm 25: 13)

> ➤ Future Prosperity   –   His   descendants   shall inherit the earth (Psalm 25:
> 13)

> ➤ Divine Confidant   – The servant of the Lord is with them (Psalm 25: 14)

> ➤ Covenant   – He will show them His covenant (Psalm 25: 14)

> ➤ Deliverance   – "He shall pluck my feet out of the net" (Psalm 25:
> 15)

The New Millionaire will always

➤ Walk in Prosperity

➤ Have New Ideas

➤ Create New Business Products

➤ Be Front Runner With Secrets Revealed

Just as God did with Abraham and with the Apostles (Genesis 18: 17 – 19 and John 15: 15)

Remember, the fear of the Lord is the beginning of wisdom. Following God's instructions to live by His word, brings great blessings!

Questions For The New Millionaire

There are many people right now, who desire to become millionaires, and as times become more difficult, that desire increases!

However, while many have this desire, there are some questions that the New Millionaire will need to ask and answer.

➤ Are you ready to take up the cross and follow Jesus?

➤ Are you ready for Him to teach you His principles – Biblical Principles – to deal with the greatest transfer of wealth about to take place? For example, Matthew 6: 33 which says – *"seek ye first the kingdom of God and His righteousness and all these things shall be added unto you"*

175

➢ Are you ready to receive 100-fold?

➢ Are you ready to invest your talents in the kingdom, for the kingdom? (Matthew 25: 14)

➢ Are you ready for the 1 hour laborers according to Matthew 20, to build the kingdom?

➢ Are you ready to submit to God's principles regarding finance found in Mark 11: 17 – 25? The Rich Young Ruler had the finance but he did not have the foundation. He loved money more than God! God wanted to teach him Kingdom Principles, that is why the Lord tested him.

Amos 8: 4 states that you ought not to practice business in such a way that it causes the poor of the land to fail. Verse 5 says,

"Saying: When will the New Moon be past, that we may sell grain? And the Sabbath, that we may trade wheat making the ephah small and the shekel large, falsifying scales by deceit."
As you observe the world today, you will realize that many of today's business people are so caught up with profit-making that they neglect everything else that brings any real value to their quality of life.

➢ They don't care about God's day of worship or observe His feast – they are only interested in is sales!

➢ They implement systems to decrease the poor, robbing them through high interest rates, sucking the poor dry of their prosperity.

➢ According to verse 6, they buy the poor for silver – little and nothing – and the needy for a pair of shoes and sell the refuse of the wealth – sell the worst

➢ Verses 7 – 8 tell that God is going to judge businessmen – including Christians.

➢ Verse 12 states that God is going to send a famine – the revelation of the Word. Businesses will only turn to those who practice Biblical Principles. The un-Godly wisdom will back fire on all the businessmen.

Amos 9: 13 gives a poetic picture of the fertility of the land and the security and stability of life for God's people, especially in His future Kingdom. Things are turning back to God's people.

"'Behold, the days are coming' says the Lord, "When the plowman shall overtake the reaper, and the treader of grapes, him who sows seed; the mountains shall drip with sweet wine, and all the hills shall flow with it.'"

The plowman versus the one who sows seed – the blessings will be so great that Amos compares them to the Lord producing so quickly and so richly that one cycle will not even be over before the next one begins!

Verse 15 declares that God will plant the people in their land, and they will never be pulled up; blessing and restoration comes with repentance first. Then God will give mercy and grace.

Mark 10: 17 speaks of the principles involved in the acquisition of Kingdom Riches - riches that will help to build the Kingdom of God.

Chapter 17

THE KEYS TO BEING A MILLIONAIRE

Keys unlock doors to numerous things and places that can bring us into great blessings. There are several keys that you need to have in order to unlock the door to *'millionaire-hood'*! Here they are:

➤ Write the vision on paper – that is – record on paper what you want to achieve. (Habakkuk 2) For example, owning your own business, house, vehicle, or plane or even having a larger number of employees!

➤ Declare *'money!'* morning and evening! Job 22: 28 tells you the power and importance of declarations. So you need to decree the following, for example, *'I am wealthy!'*; *'I am a multi-billionaire!'*; *'I am blessed coming in and blessed going out!'* (Job 21: 28); According to Proverbs 18: 21, I declare that my hands are blessed and my businesses are blessed.

➤ Be humble; remain humble; and declare that exaltation will come! Even if you have been cast down by business partners and enemies! When you do Job 22: 29 says *'...then HE will save the humble...'*

➤ Develop a hate for poverty! Poverty brings destruction to the poor. (Proverbs 10:15)

➢ Always sow seed! (Genesis 8: 22; Ecclesiastes 11: 4 – 6) For every request you put before God, seal it with a seed. Don't withhold your hand. Proverbs 11: 24 – 26 reveal that generosity prospers a person, and also that stinginess brings poverty.

➢ Study the word of God regarding prosperity and direction, as well as the various seeds for the various problems. For example, II Chronicles 1 reveals the $1000 Solomonic Seed for Business; Psalm 112 Seed of $112 for Wealth and Riches; and the Psalm 119 Seed of $119 for Direction!

➢ Pay your Tithes, according to Malachi 3: 10 and observe the Three (3) Feasts as in Exodus 23: 14 – 19. In addition to this, practice the Firstfruits Principle; the firstfruits belong to the priest. For example, blessing the priest with the increase of your salary (the difference between your old and new salaries). The firstfruits ultimately belong to God!

➢ Practice Biblical Principles according to Deuteronomy 14: 22 – 29, because this will allow the Lord to bless you in all the work of your hands which you do. That is the key to becoming a millionaire. Do not forsake the Levites – your pastors within your gates as well as your Government, Church, Community, and City must be first. Additionally, Deuteronomy 14: 29 tells us to help the strangers, the fatherless, widows, and pastors within your gates from the blessing you receive; so that the Lord will bless all the work of your hand. If all the Churches and Businesses were applying this principle, God would bless them mightily!

Recognize that in order to be a millionaire:

➢ You must be able to discern market conditions. For example, Joseph, Elijah and Solomon got fresh revelation for solutions.

➢ You must be willing to obey God's instruction when He speaks, as it admonishes us in Deuteronomy 28: 1.

➢ Always remember Deuteronomy 8. Meditate on it and you will prosper. Additionally, keep Deuteronomy 28: 1 - 14 close to your heart and you will prosper.

Remember:

➢ Do not associate with negative people, especially those with negative views toward money. Associate instead with people who love to talk about God and money. Having God and money will bring happiness and joy.

➢ Lack of money brings stress, debt, sickness, poverty and lack of opportunity.

➢ Create a budget and present it to God. Write down the amount you are looking for yearly on a blank check and put it on the wall of your prayer room. It will come to pass! Faith without works is dead – James 2: 14 – 26.

➤ Don't just sit, try different businesses. God cannot open to you His good treasure or give the rain to your land and bless all the work of your hand unless you put your hand to something.

➤ Seek the Lord to find out with whom you are really called to do business. Wrong associations and affiliations can bring you into poverty.

➤ Put up signs in your home with Scriptures regarding money and wealth confessions. This is prophetic!

Trading – Luke 19: 11 – 26

For expansion and increase, you must first be faithful with the little, before God gives you authority over other cities! In addition to this you must increase by trading what you were given, and at least double that. Failure to invest what God has given you and doubling it will incur God's judgement. Also, He deems you a wicked servant. Failure to invest and trade will be taken away and given to others. God is in the kingdom business.

In the Bible you see the following person's involved in trading. Look at Abraham in Genesis 13: 2. Solomon was also one involved in trading. Trading can simply be an exchange in assets, loan of goods, money, silver or gold with interest. Trading is what allowed Joseph to be great. He was trading in slavery for money.

Sowing seed, according to Genesis 8: 22, is also trading, because there will always be a guaranteed harvest of more than you have sown. It is increase on your seed; one seed can bring forth millions of seed.

Solomon traded food and oil for cedar and cypress logs to build the temple, according to I Kings 5: 2 – 9. Year by year, many nations needed to start to trade with other nations to beat the economic recession.

This therefore means that the Church can trade also with business people via

> ➢ The teaching of Biblical Principles

> ➢ Networking with other organizations such as banks

> ➢ Housing

> ➢ Schools

Charitable Deeds

Now there are several keys to follow when you are doing charitable deeds. Abide by Matthew 6:

> ➢ Do not do deeds in order to be seen by men otherwise you will have no rewards from the Father in heaven.

➤ Do not sound a trumpet before you as the hypocrites do in the synagogues and in the street as they are looking for glory from men.

➤ When you are giving, do not let your left hand know what your right hand is doing. God will reward you openly when you do it in secret.

Jesus in Luke 19: 28 – 34 sent His disciples to loose a colt for His ministry. (See also Matthew 21: 1 – 4)

Use the two (2) golden keys to fight to get prosperity – **bind** all negative forces, spirits and words spoken against your finance and **loose** millions to you – Matthew 16: 19 and Matthew 18: 18.

The power of agreement is the key to loose wealth, according to Matthew 18: 19 – 20 and I Corinthians 1: 10, especially with husbands and wives. This also applies to business partners.

The Holy Spirit Is Key

Now, by reading Isaiah 32: 15 – 18, you will realize that if nations, organizations and individuals, particularly business people are to walk in wealth and prosperity, they must pray that the Holy Spirit will pour out upon them. The Holy Spirit is the source of all blessing in the End Times. The Holy Spirit is the Key for Justice, Righteousness, and Peaceful, Ethical Existence.

Isaiah 32: 19 – 20 also speak even in disaster or God's judgement on a nation or city. Verse 20 specifically tells us *"Blessed are you who sow beside all waters; who send out freely the feet of the ox and the donkey."*

Isaiah 30: 23 – 24 say *"He will give the rain for your seed."*

Despite judgement, God will bless those who sow seed. He will give the rain for your seed.

In order to be a millionaire, you have to follow protocol of communication to get or understand the mysteries of God. I Corinthians 14: 2, mysteries for wealth and other vital areas will only be revealed through the *"heavenly language"* – study more closely the word *'mysteries'* which means *'secrets'*.

In addition to that, to be a millionaire, you must put God first in every aspect. You cannot give priority to your personal needs, businesses and so on, while you ignore God's house. That will bring hardship on you and on the nation – Haggai 1: 1 – 11.

Haggai 1: 10 states that God will withhold the dew and the earth withhold its fruit. When the earth withholds its fruit, then:

➢ Famine

➢ Drought

➢ Food Shortage

➢ Failed Investments

Haggai 2: 17 states that God struck all the labors of your hand - the business transactions, investments - because He wants you to acknowledge Him as the One who has blessed you and causes the rain to fall; so that you will begin to build His temple and to give your money and you heart.

God will bless His people's seed of obedience, according to Haggai 2: 19. However, the same principles that apply when you neglect or refuse to Tithe apply also when you do not pay your taxes, according to Malachi 3: 10 and Matthew 22: 21. There is a delinquency period and a charge.

Always remember, according to Matthew 15: 13, whatever the Father did not plant in a nation or an economy, will be uprooted. You must also declare blessings each day on your life. This will cancel out all the curses of your enemies. For example, Galatians 5: 22 – 23 speak of the nine (9) fruits of the spirit which will bring harvest.

The number '9' means *'harvest; fruitfulness'*

Having the *'fruit'* will allow you to walk into wealth and maintain it. Pray also, according to Isaiah 11: 2, for the seven Spirits, which is still the Holy Spirit:

➢ Spirit of the Lord
➢ Spirit of Wisdom
➢ Spirit of Understanding
➢ Spirit of Counsel
➢ Spirit of Might
➢ Spirit of Knowledge

➢ Spirit of the Fear Of The Lord

The number '7' means '*complete rest*'

All leaders need these seven (7) ministries in order to effectively lead a nation or any organization.

➢ Never go before any king without bringing a gift, as is stated in Matthew 2: 11. When you give a king a gift, He will give you gifts/favor, power/authority, or kingly impartation. God has given/sown His Son to redeem His family that mankind can live.

➢ Edify yourself concerning how to understand God's word and how to receive revelation regarding prosperity – I Corinthians 14: 4. Take special note of the word '*edify*'.

➢ Always practice forgiveness of others, especially if someone gives you a debt write-off. As you have been shown compassion and given a debt release, you must now pass it on to someone who is indebted to you. This principle is clearly revealed in Matthew 18: 21 - 35

- Step 1:   Debt Release

- Step 2:   Forgiveness

The New Millionaire should not indulge in un-Godly counsel, as is stated in Psalm 1: 1.

"Blessed is the man who walks not in the counsel of the un-Godly"

Remember that according to Proverbs 10: 22, it is the blessings of the Lord that makes one rich, and He adds no sorrow to it. God's blessing allows you to be a millionaire – no one or nothing else. You need God's blessings to be a millionaire. Once God releases it, then it will be so.

In order for you to be great, God has to bless you greatly. This is expressed in Genesis 24: 35 when Abraham's servant Eliezer described his master's wealth. In addition to that Genesis 13: 2 tells us that

'Abraham was very rich in livestock, in silver and in gold.'

A millionaire should be constructively critical of certain things using Biblical criteria. For example, they ought to be concerned with and knowledgeable of those that will marry their son or daughter. Marrying the wrong person will bring you back into poverty.

Abraham was a billionaire and well advanced in years according to Genesis 24: 3 when he instructed his servant Eliezer:

"and I will make you swear by the Lord, the God of heaven and the God of the earth, that you will not take a wife for my son from the daughters of the Canaanites, among whom I dwell;"

The *'Canaanites'* here in our day would refer to those who are *'unsaved'* or *'not of the same (Christian) faith'*.

As a result, Rebekah married a billionaire– Isaac, son of Abraham, and became part of the Abrahamic Promise.

There is nothing more important than the blessing of the Lord to us. Abraham knew this and because of his faith and obedience to God, he maintained it all the days of his life and it continued down the lineage with Isaac.

When the Lord is blessing you, according to Genesis 24: 40, He will always send the angels assigned to bring prosperity to go before you, to make your way prosperous. You must pray that the Lord will send the prosperity angels before us! (See also Exodus 23: 20, 23 & 30; Joshua 24: 8)

The enemy is afraid that God's people will get wealth that is why God has to send prosperity angels before us to inherit the land – our inheritance. But God wants us to obey His word so that He may release wealth, according to Joshua 1: 7 – 9, especially verse 8.

The New Millionaire must know Genesis 12: 2, that God will bless us to be a blessing (to others). Genesis 12: 3 tells us that God will:

"... bless those who bless you, and I will curse him who curses you ..."

Therefore, if you curse a blessed man, you will be cursed! But further to this, when you are blessed, your families, your church and all who bless you will be blessed. (See also Galatians 3: 8). Don't ask for a blessing unless you are going to bless others.

According Genesis 12: 1 – 2, each time God is going to bless you and use you and allow you to be great:

> ➤ He removes you from your father's house

> ➤ He removes you from your country and kindred (See also Genesis 13: 9; Acts 7: 2 – 3)

> ➤ He gets you in a place that was predestined from the beginning

> ➤ He then establishes you there (See also Deuteronomy 26: 5)

> ➤ He then blesses you (See also Genesis 22: 17 – 18)

> ➤ Your name will then become great and famous

> ➤ Then you shall be a blessing to others (See also Genesis 28: 3 – 4)

Based on the various dimensions a person can be a blessing, but not reach the heights of being a blessing to others. Being a blessing to others, according Genesis 12: 2, is a blessing from God, in the same way that giving is a gift.

Abraham's covenant is three-fold:

> ➤ Blessings for those people and nations that bless Abraham and for the nations that come from him, which means that you and your seed are also entitled to the same blessing – spiritually and naturally.

> ➤ Curses upon those people and nations which curse Abraham and Israel, that means the curses will come upon those that curse you and your seed also.

> ➤ Blessing on all the families of the earth through Jesus Christ

Exodus 23: 30 says:

"Little by little I will drive them out from before you, until you have increase and you inherit the land."

To be a millionaire you must have a millionaire mindset. Don't think small, think BIG! In order to get wisdom, associate with the wealthy – go where they go! Don't be stingy and don't refuse to spend in order to get wisdom. Those who don't have the millionaire mindset ultimately lack faith and trust in God.

This is the greatest time in history to be a millionaire, while the earth become darker, God is ready to transfer the wealth to the *'just'*, that is, those who are ready to abide by His principles and be kingdom-minded, will rise quickly to millionaire status. (See Job 27: 16 – 17)

According to Genesis 26: 12 – 14, when you sow during a famine you get:

> ➢ Higher returns on your investment (your seed)

> ➢ 100-fold return in the same year

> ➢ The blessing of the Lord

> ➢ A 3-fold blessing

The Laws Of Access And The New Millionaire

The New Millionaire must pray for the three-tiered Law of Access. Once God gives you the Law of Access, which are:

> ➢ The Law of Access

> ➢ The Law of Presentation

> ➢ The Law of Favor

- then numerous doors will open.

Further to this, there are several things to keep in mind regarding the Law of Access.

> ➢ Access is the key to promotion

> ➢ Access to God will give you access to man

➢ Who sees you determines who promotes you. Joseph was promoted through this Law of Access. He was recommended by the Chief Butler (Pharaoh's Butler) in Genesis 41: 9.

➢ Your gift will take you to great men as it was with Joseph in Genesis 41: 9 – 15

➢ The slave girl allowed Elisha's access to Naaman, the commander of the army

➢ A blind man fought to get access to Jesus in order to be healed in John 5: 1 – 13

➢ The access that Elijah had to the widow opened doors for both in I Kings 17: 9 – 24

➢ All things that you are praying for are behind a door. Write a list of the people to whom you want to have access so that your God-given vision can be fulfilled.

➢ When God gives access, don't allow a third voice/party to break that access. Make a list of the people to whom you want access in order to fulfill your God-given vision

➢ Ruth's obedience to Naomi's instruction caused her to meet and marry Boaz, a wealthy man of royal lineage, and to become the grandmother of one of Israel's greatest kings.

The Law of Presentation

How you present yourself, your ministry and your products is a key element in the Law of Presentation.

In marketing, even bad products will sell if it is properly packaged. Proper packaging will catch the attention of investors quickly. It will also increase awareness of what you have to offer and bring about greater attraction to you, your ministry or your product.

The Law of Favor

This Law is based generally on Psalm 5: 12. There are several interesting Scriptures of which you must take note concerning the Law of Favor.

- ➢ Favor from God will cause you to one day be a millionaire – Proverbs 12: 2

- ➢ Joseph rose from rags to riches in one day because of the favor of God on his life – Genesis 41: 42

- ➢ Favor is greater than money! Favor is for life! Psalm 30: 5

- ➢ You need favor from God and man; Abraham, Moses, David, and Joseph all found favor with God and man – Daniel 1

In order to be a millionaire, you need God's favor in every area – body, soul and spirit!

What The New Millionaire Must Understand

The New Millionaire must understand that the successes that he/she released in the past and releases in the present are the blessings of God, according to Deuteronomy 8: 18. Further to this, Job was a multi-millionaire and his prosperity was a direct result of His lifestyle of piety and benevolence. He gave, and according to Job 29: 11 – 17, God wants the New Millionaire to give so his/her their prosperity will continue.

Always remember:

➤ According to Job 29: 1 – 2, it is God who protects you and it is His Light that is carrying you through darkness

➤ It is the friendly counsel of God that is over your business or home so that He may bring you into prosperity – Job 29: 4

Millionaires must know that uncommon favor will dry up when God observes greed, as is found in Malachi 3: 8 – 9. Once you cease paying Tithes because of greed, it affects you and your business, your household or your nation. The favor you once received to make major profit will no longer be extended to you!

Luke 2: 52 further reveals that God is the One Who gives favor to increase in wisdom as well as favor with man and every other thing you have.

Chapter 18

THE THINGS EVERY MILLIONAIRE NEEDS TO UNDERSTAND

There are a few things that every millionaire **must** understand in order to be a good steward of what God has or will bless you with – Riches, Wealth and The Big 3!

<u>Riches</u>

The term *'riches'* is used to speak of *'the blessings of God in Christian life'*. There are different categories of Riches.

> ➤ Riches of His Goodness   -   Romans 2: 4

> ➤ Riches of His Glory   -   Romans 9: 23

> ➤ Riches of His Grace   -   Ephesians 1: 7
> Ephesians 2: 7

> ➤ Riches of His Wisdom
> and Knowledge   -   Romans 11: 23

> ➤ Riches of Christ   -   Ephesians 3: 8

> ➤ Riches of His Presence   -   Colossians 1: 27

> ➤ Riches of His Reproach   -   Hebrews 11: 26

> ➤ Riches of the Gentiles   -   Romans 11: 12

There is nothing wrong with wealth; as long as you do not allow the danger of being consumed by it or of wrongfully using it to take the forefront. Riches should be used to build God's Kingdom first and then to help the poor, fatherless and widow. God wants you to seek for the spiritual riches before the natural, so that you will have the necessary wisdom to distribute and manage, and that God will be glorified through your wealth. You must pray that He will bless you so that you can be a blessing to others and worship Him with your riches!

Wealth

The term *'wealth'* means *'riches, abundant possessions'* and *'the state of being rich'*.

Wealth can be used in different ways, spiritually or naturally. Earthly possessions relate to different classes of people.

Those who are rich in the things of the earth and poor in spiritual assets – according to Luke 16: 19 – 31 & Luke 12: 13 – 21, are not interested in the things of God. This kind of poverty will lead you to hell!

Poverty is a spirit that carries two (2) functions:

> To attack God's people and drain them of the earthly riches, this can cause death or prevent them from achieving certain goals and so on

> Further to this it deceives the rich into walking in poverty of the things of God. This poverty will end them in hell, as they have no riches in glory!

Dives was rich with earthly things, but was poor in the things of God and that spirit of poverty landed him in hell! It is better that you walk in poverty in earthly things and be rich in the things of God, than vice versa, just as was the case with Lazarus the beggar.

The 'Big 3'

The 'Big 3' refers to the three (3) main issues that affect mankind! They are:

> Lack of Finance (Money)

> Relationships and Sex

> Sickness

If the new millionaire can recognize these problems and how to overcome them, and then apply the solutions to his/her life, then he/she will become ten times wiser in how to acquire and maintain his/her blessings!

When you face these three (3) issues, then you must also recognize and accept the following:

> More seeking is required of you. According to Matthew 6: 33, you must seek God even more deeply concerning these areas as they all relate to
>

the Kingdom, that He may lead you to the
solutions.

➢ Because of the potential that exists when you have
your health, finances and relationships in line
according to Biblical Principles, the enemy fights
you, because these tools are the most powerful
against the kingdom of darkness. It means that
with these intact, God will get the glory and the
people of God will be victorious – so He fights!

The First Issue - Money

The enemy always tries to get you to speak negatively
about money particularly as it concerns Christians or the
Church! So you are automatically positioned incorrectly
on a mental and spiritual level to receive wealth or to get
rich. You must understand and accept the fact that God
wants you to have riches and wealth, but with a
Kingdom-building, Gospel-spreading mindset; along
with the zeal to accomplish great things to His honor and
glory with such wealth and riches!

In the midst of this, you must recognize the principles
that can help you to get on the right track concerning
money – spiritually and naturally:

➢ Seed, Time and Harvest (Genesis 8: 26)

➢ Biblical Principles for Wealth Building (Malachi 3)

➢ Proper Allocation of our Money (Deuteronomy 8)

➢ Ignorance of how to tap into the anointing of the man of God! (II Chronicles 9; I Kings 10: 1 – 13)

Recognize that the only time God's people are not happy is when it comes to giving MONEY! But you must recognize that giving is a part of worship.

The Second Issue – Relationships/Sex

This is an issue that many don't believe has anything to do with your success in any area because as far as they are concerned, the issue of sex and those with whom you enter into personal relationships is a private matter. However, your disobedience in the area of Sexual Relationships and Family affects everything you are connected to including your finances!

The key thing to remember is that once you break one of God's Principles or Commands, the devil then has a legal right to attack you in any area he chooses!

Many persons:

➢ Lack the knowledge of Biblical Principles regarding relationships and sex

➢ Are afraid to discuss the topic of Sex

> Did not use the right method in choosing a life partner – they did not employ Biblical Principles in doing so. (Proverbs 31)

> Do not know each other's role from a Biblical Standpoint

> Don't know what Jesus says about it and the Church according to Ephesians 5

> Lack submission – the wives don't submit to their husbands and the husbands refuse to submit to God!

> Are experiencing problems because of a lack of money so they cannot enjoy life properly or with each other as they would like.

Some of these things may seem insignificant and even controversial, but they matter to God and often determine the extent of His blessings upon you.

The Third Issue – Sickness

Many persons who are sick today would give a million dollars just to have their health restored!

Our health is important to God and is directly connected to the health of our souls!

Here are a number of reasons for ill-health:

> - To bring even greater glory to God. (The Entire Book Of Job)

> - Sexual Sins – including Fornication, Adultery and Perversion

> - Wrong Exposure to Sex and Soul Ties

> - Being connected to the wrong family lineage – especially through marriage

> - Not eating right i.e. Biblically

> - Lack of knowledge of witchcraft and spiritual warfare

> - Disobedience to God (Deuteronomy 7: 15; Exodus 15: 26)

> - Generational Curses (Exodus 34: 7)

> - Lack of Finance to allow you to take proper care of your body

> - Lack of knowledge of the word of God particularly concerning demonic activity (Mark 5)

> - Lack of knowledge about the contents, nutritive value and details of the foods you eat

> - Lack of knowledge of the importance of Water intake

> ➢ Lack of understanding about proper nutrition

> ➢ Lack of understanding of the Holy Spirit

> ➢ Lack of knowledge of the Power of God's Word

From this you can determine yourselves what to do on our part to prevent sickness!

Now the number one reason for God to bless you both spiritually and naturally, for example with Spiritual gifts, the Anointing in and for business, or with money or real estate and more assets, is for the growth of the church which leads to the building of the Kingdom of God!
God wants you to be a blessing to others. Recognize, therefore, that:

> ➢ God gives you favor because He wants you to favor others

> ➢ God gives you Riches and access to Finance because He wants you to help others with Finance

> ➢ God opens doors for you because He wants to use you to open doors for others

Psalm 34 is a good Scripture to look at regarding all this as it gives us instructions on how to get happiness and blessings!

> ➢ **Verse 4** – tells you to seek the Lord and He will hear you and deliver you from all your fears.

➢ **Verse 6** – tells you of the poor who cried out and the Lord heard him, and saved him out of all his troubles. Evidently God will do the same for you!

➢ **Verse 7** – tells of God's protection and security for those who fear Him!

➢ **Verse 8** – tells of the blessings and testimony for those who trust in God.

➢ **Verse 9 & 10** – says that those who fear and seek the Lord shall not lack any good thing!

➢ **Verse 15 – 17** – says that God's eyes are always on the righteous and His ears are open to their cry.

➢ **Verse 18** – says that He is near to those who have a broken heart and saves those who have a contrite spirit!

➢ **Verse 22** – says He redeems the souls of His servants and that none that trust in Him shall be condemned!

Power to obtain genuine prosperity resides only in the Gospel of Christ.

III John verse 2 tells you that God prays:

"… that you may prosper in all things and be in health, just as your soul prospers"

God wants it, but He knows that it will not happen to all, because there is a lack of knowledge and seeking of Him.

As you look into all of this, you must also understand that not all prosperity comes from God! Some prosperity is counterfeit and is designed for you to lose your way to God and come to utter shame! That is the enemy's plan! But only God, and all He encompasses, are genuine and will stand! The counterfeit will not last.

And so, according to Genesis 50: 20 remember that whatever was meant evil God will turn around for your good, and that according to Romans 8: 28, that all things work together for good to them that love the Lord, God will cause some of this wealth that has been gained by unjust means to be turned over to His people for the purpose of Kingdom-building and to reveal His strength as the true and living God!

Remember that God wants you to prosper spiritually and physically. Matthew 6: 33 reminds you that the more you seek Him first, the richer you will become spiritually and physically, and all other things will be added to you also!

It is God that gives the power to get wealth – Deuteronomy 8: 18 – and He teaches you to profit – Isaiah 48: 17. He will lead you the way you should go. For example, He will direct you in investment give you business ideas, guidance and open the doors to networking and connections with the right people!

God Speaks To Mankind

From time to time, people will say, "Did God say so?" or "Did God speak?" Others will say, "God never said that to anybody; you're telling me what you think?" or "That is gibberish, nothing goes like that!" Even better, "God does not work like that."

So the question is, does God communicate with man? Only someone who is dead is unable to speak. Is God dead?

Any teacher, professor or leader of an organisation will tell you that communication is a two-way process, and is not complete without a response of some kind.

Many times we hear persons say, "Something tells me I shouldn't do this" or "My mind is telling me not to take this bus" or "Don't go on the corner today"; only to realize that when you obey, something terrible had happened there, and you were saved from it. So, who spoke?

How God Speaks

God speaks in dreams and visions, (Genesis 20:6; Matthew 1:19-21) through the written word, directly in a still, small voice – face to face or in dark speeches, (Numbers 12:6-8; I Kings 19:12) or He uses His servants to speak to you (those who serve Him faithfully). God will even use a donkey to speak to you (Numbers 22:24-27). He will use the elements (atmospheric conditions); and He will speak to you through your circumstances.

Job 33:14-16 says, "For God may speak in one way, or in another, yet man does not perceive it. In a dream, in a vision of the night, when deep sleep falls upon men, while slumbering on their beds, then He opens the ears of men, and seals their instruction."

God shows leaders various symbols, even in their dreams, to allow them to lead effectively. For example, many of those who dispute the fact that God still speaks, are among the first to run to the horoscopes, psychics, tarot readers, tea leaf readers or listen to old wives' tales. The question is, with whom are they communicating when they go there?

The very rainbow we see from time to time is communication from God, reminding us of the Covenant He made with man on the earth (Genesis 9:13-16).

The very color of the grass is often a reflection of what is happening in a nation. An animal's response to its instinct warns man about what is happening in the atmosphere. When certain ants begin to dig up the dirt, we realize that rain is coming. When we see the ants in a long line storing up their food, you know that there are hard times ahead. Before the tsunami in Thailand, (2006) all the animals ran to the hills and many wondered why; it was the sign of an impending disaster.

God speaks also to the meteorologists (Matthew 16: 1-4). When God does something atmospherically, they are being given the message for the people through the weather. They report the weather and give forecasts, but they cannot discern the meaning of what they are seeing so they cannot accurately inform the people.

When people say God spoke to them, the first thing they will hear is that they are fanatics or that they are paranoid or even schizophrenic. Some engage in phone bugging, secret tape recordings and computer hacking to get information. They trust the computer more than they are willing to spend time and listen to God.

Hearing His Voice

Our inability to hear God's voice can be costly. It causes us to make wrong choices, poor decisions, deception, defeat, delay and death. A number of politicians, administrations and organizations are no more, because of their inability or refusal to listen when God speaks.

Hearing God's voice daily will bring growth, increase, promotion and blessing. It will also save lives. It is critical for all individuals and national leaders, before making any major decisions, to seek to hear what God is communicating about it.

Whatever deals, agreements, activities, policies, reformations, laws, constitutional changes, or moves there are to be made, we must listen to the voice of God first and know what He is saying about them, so we can make the right decisions for the benefit of all.

Chapter 19

DON'T TRUST IN RICHES

Trust In God And Sow Your Seed
Mark 10: 17-22

God says in Exodus 20: 3:

"You shall have no other gods before Me."

This is the first of the ten (10) utterances (commandments) of God! Whatever you revere more than God becomes an idol. For example, if your trust in, and commitment to riches and wealth are greater than your commitment to and love for God, then God is not first in your life and your wealth and riches have become your gods.

You need to ask the question and see if you spend more time getting riches rather than spending time before God. Ask yourself how many hours you spend at work and on anything else for that matter. Then ask yourself how many hours you spend with God. Are you devoting enough time to God? Where does your loyalty lie? Remember the first Commandment!

There are many people who say that they are following the Commandments of God as in Mark 10: 19:

"You know the commandments: 'Do not commit adultery, Do not murder, Do not steal, Do not bear false witness, Do not defraud, honor you father and your mother.'"

They fail to do so because they lack whole-hearted allegiance to God.

Jesus gave the rich young ruler a test to show him that he had made an idol of his wealth. There is no one who can say he/she is keeping the Commandments, when he/she is more loyal to wealth, power, jobs, and even to people.

In order to inherit the kingdom, you must be able to be whole-heartedly committed to God. That's the only way to be willing to take up the cross. For the rich to inherit the kingdom, they have to be ready to depart with their wealth if asked to do so to follow God.

Mark 10: 22 reveals, many would rather go to hell, than give up their possessions. Also, Mark 8: 37 tells us it does not make sense to gain the world and lose your soul.

In verses 23 – 24, Jesus says it is hard for those who trust in riches to enter the Kingdom of God. Now in the kingdom of God there are many benefits:

> ➢ Everlasting Life

> ➢ Protection

> ➢ Healing

> ➢ Prosperity in all areas (especially their souls)

> ➢ Joy

> ➢ Peace

➤ Happiness

➤ God's Power

God wants the rich to enjoy all the benefits of the kingdom while they are rich. However, most commit their trust to their riches rather than to God. Hence, it is difficult to enter the Kingdom of God.

In Mark 10: 28, Peter outlined that they have left all to follow Jesus. He outlined that those who give up all for His sake will get good returns on their investment – that they have invested in Him.

Investment in the Kingdom will yield the highest profit payout and the value of your harvest will not depreciate. Instead you will receive a hundred fold return on:

➤ Houses and Real Estate

➤ Families and Relatives (spiritual and natural)

➤ Lands

➤ Eternal Life is key

Blessings that Jesus gives us will far outweigh material loss and persecution incurred in service to him. II Chronicles 25: 9 speaks of God's unlimited resources.

In man's economy, the law of supply and demand regulates the price paid for goods and services. In times of oversupply, the prices go down, in times of shortage the prices rise. Man's economy fluctuates with times and seasons.

God's economy has no shortages – supply always equals our needs.

He does not want any of His people to have any lack; but rather have continual increase according to I Thessalonians 4: 10 – 12. God always multiplies what you give to Him.

In Matthew 17: 19 – 20 you will see that the disciples could not cure the child; they did not have the anointing to do so. In order to get the anointing there must be a seed sown; even a seed as small as a mustard seed. Only when you sow a seed can you truly speak to the mountain in your life.

The mountain can be:

➢ Adversity

➢ Sin

➢ Sickness

➢ Demons

➢ Diseases

anything that hinders you from getting the anointing.

Note that the mustard seed is very small; but even a small seed can move huge mountains. Jesus was teaching the disciples about the importance of seed faith to move mountain. For example, it could be lack of faith. When fear comes, sow to deal with it. Sow seed and nothing will be impossible to you.

A non-sower will not walk in certain levels of anointing; and someone who walks in unbelief in sowing seed will not walk in the anointing. God says sow a seed and speak to your mountain and God will remove it.

Again, the seeds of:

➤ $17.20 from Matthew 17: 20 is the *'Mustard Seed'* Seed

➤ $32.15 from Jeremiah 32: 9 – 15 for Deeds/Houses/Fields/Vineyards

He used the number '17' – as in 17 shekels of silver – to purchase deeds.

As small a seed as $17.20, from Matthew 17: 20 can give you a miracle of any kind and move huge mountains. This seed will remove stumbling blocks, demons and any other kind of mountain in your life.

Genesis 37: 2 tells us that Joseph was 17 years old when he got the dream of greatness.

The number '20' means **'holy; tried and approved'** according to Revelation 4:4

Now John 10: 10 reveals that God desires abundance, and he desires to give His children abundance. The enemy always wants to rob you of God's blessings, oppress your bodies and destroy everything that you love. However, you can stop him by living right and sowing seed. The devil knows that many of God's people walk in unbelief regarding Seed Time and Harvest and are afraid to sow!

Jesus knows that there are different categories of seed; but He challenged that they must sow even the smallest seed – even a mustard seed – because even the small seed can create a miracle and remove mountains!

Riches Cannot Redeem - Psalm 49

By now, you ought to realize that wealth and riches cannot redeem anyone, hence, you cannot put your trust in them.

Now, the word *'redeem'* means *'to buy back, recover by expenditure of effort or by a stipulated payment; make a single payment to discharge convert tokens or bonds and so on into goods or cash; of God or Christ deliver from ... and damnation; save rescue or reclaim.'*

The writer says that those who trust in their wealth and boast in the multitude of their riches – none can save his brother or pay God a ransom that his soul will not go to hell if he is not saved.

Money cannot buy life. When it comes time to die, no modern medicine and all the money in the world can stop death. Verses 14 - 15 reveal that riches in life do not have the final word – GOD DOES!

When a righteous man dies, He shall have dominion over death! God will redeem his soul from the power of the grave. God shall receive him.

God does not want anyone to be afraid when he or she becomes rich. When the glory of His house is increased – *'Glory'* is symbolic of wealth with its high social status. No one can carry anything with him/her when he/she dies. A man who has earthly honor but does not have God, is nothing! He will be as it is stated in verse 20:

"A man who is in honor yet does not understand is like the beasts that perish".

The impressive man who does not operate within the spirit realm will die with no more advantage than an animal. Failure of the rich man to accept Christ means that he shall never see the light.

Chapter 20

FASTING: THE NEW MILLIONAIRE'S GREATEST SECRET WEAPON

Fasting is one of the most effective weapons for any person to use. There are many different kinds of Fasts that are used to deal with problems and crises in business, individual health issues, and for the purpose of protection or for breakthrough! In fact, certain breakthroughs cannot happen without Fasting and Prayer.

As millionaires, you cannot achieve certain kinds of breakthrough without Fasting.

There are seven (7) Biblical Fasts that you can do in order to receive breakthroughs. Jesus taught His disciples to Fast! In Matthew 6: 16 – 17 He instructs us to:

✓ Wash our face and

✓ Anoint our head!

The Seven (7) Main Fasts

THE FAST	LENGTH OF FAST	THE SCRIPTURE	THE PURPOSE
Esther Fast	3 Days – No food or Water*	Esther 4: (esp. 16)	This is the Fast for Crises and to bring you great Favor and Protection. This Fast also averts any plots against you!
Daniel Fast	10 Days – Vegetables and Water only!	Daniel 1: 9 - 21	To prove God in your favor For better appearance Weight Increase Success in Interviews and with Big Deals For Knowledge and Skills in all literature For increase in Godly wisdom Interpretation in Dreams and Visions To be 10 times better than the opposition or any other realm which is not of God!

THE FAST	LENGTH OF FAST	THE SCRIPTURE	THE PURPOSE
21-Day Fast (Daniel)	21 Days – Water & Vegetables Only!	Daniel 10: 2 - 3	This Fast will bring divine revelation in different ways regarding: 1. New business 2. Things coming 3. How to invest It will also release the blessings that the enemy has been and/or is holding up from you. There are always evil, spiritual forces that hinder our blessings. This fast also reveals the interpretation of those things that God would reveal.
3-Day Fast	3 Days – No Meat!	I Samuel 30: 11 - 12	This Fast is for Physical Healing and it also helps the body to eliminate toxins and promote good health!

THE FAST	LENGTH OF FAST	THE SCRIPTURE	THE PURPOSE
Isaiah 58 Fast	1 Day: 6 am - 6 pm	Isaiah 58	Before Fasting: There must be Repentance (whether by Individuals and Nations). Loose the bonds of wickedness To undo the heavy burdens To let the oppressed go free To break the heavy yoke For Healing (Individuals or Nations) Protection and Blessing For God to answer Petitions. Deliverance from Political, Economic and Social Injustice. Guidance Provision Restoration Building and Re-development Light and Growth Justice Prosperity Righteousness and Holiness

THE FAST	LENGTH OF FAST	THE SCRIPTURE	THE PURPOSE
Consecration Fast	3 or 7 Days – No meat, no sweet	Joel 1: 13-14	This Fast is for nations, churches, businesses and these organizations would need to set aside time for this purpose. They would close down operations for Consecration. This Fast must be done by the priest for the nations and also the church, especially when the blessings are withheld from the House of God. God wants them to Fast and Pray all night that the resources will return. The church leaders must gather all the assembly to deal with corporate sin in the Church and the Nation. Famine is judgement from God! Crime, violence, poor economic conditions, are also examples of judgement from God. Fires burning and consuming property and acres of land, shortage of water, drying up of lakes, springs, rivers are judgement from God! This Fast will turn things around in the Church and in the Nations! What happens in the nations affects the church, but the Church has the key to direct the nations!

THE FAST	LENGTH OF FAST	THE SCRIPTURE	THE PURPOSE
Repentance Fast	1 – 7 Days – No meat, No Sweet	Joel 2: 12	For Individuals, Nations, Churches and Businesses! Repentance is the key to prosperity. Each time God wants to bless His people He always calls them to repentance. God cares about His people. That is why He says in John 10: 10 "The thief does not come except to steal, and to kill, and to destroy. I have come that they may have life and they may have it more **abundantly."

** 'Abundantly' means 'excessively, overflowing, surplus, over and above, more than enough, more than sufficient, extra-ordinarily or above the ordinary!

More About the Joel 2 Fast

God's plan from the beginning was for man to be enriched and to have a prosperous, abundant life. Each time God wants to bless, He says you must turn to Him with all your hearts, with fasting, weeping and mourning.

Verse 14 shows the goodness of God! God always wants to bless you even in our sinful state; but as you repent, **"He will turn and relent, and leave a blessing behind Him – A grain offering and a drink offering for the Lord your God?"**

God wants you to repent, He does not want the world to rule over you, you are His and He loves you!

This Joel 2 (Repentance) Fast will bring benefits according to verse 18.

> ➢ The Lord will be refreshed

> ➢ The Lord will be zealous for His land and pity His people

And according to verse 19 He will:

"… answer and say to His people 'Behold I send you grain, new wine and oil…'"

This means provision, prosperity, revival in business, nations, churches – you cannot survive without God's Spirit and His blessings.

> ➢ He will lift up His people and His people will no longer be a reproach!

> ➢ God will remove the dead things; the things that ravish our economy, business, profits and so on! Loss will be no more.

> ➤ There will be growth, new business ideas, restoration of things that were stolen, lost or dead, whether in businesses, churches or nations!

> ➤ Even the beasts will not be afraid because the famine will not affect them.

> ➤ The pastures will also spring up again!

> ➤ It will be harvest time again – the former rain! This means that there will be heavenly downpours of blessings, prosperity, wisdom, spiritual manifestation and growth in all areas!

God is not just going to give you past blessings but these former blessings will overtake you! Major increase, growth, development and wealth will be experienced!

Understand that the term *'Former Rain'* refers to the autumn rain which coincides with planting time. On the other hand, the 'Latter Rain' is the spring rain that occurs just before the harvest – the outpouring of refreshing rain which renews the fertility of the parched ground! From a spiritual standpoint, as you make reference to these terms, they speak to the outpouring of the Spirit of God which brings Spiritual renewal in you!

The Holy Spirit is the key to bring prosperity to a nation, an individual or to businesses. All God wants is that you go into repentance, fast, cry out, and turn from your sinful direction and be blessed by Him. Then after this He will do the major outpouring, through dreams, visions, divine revelation, prophecy, and so on. Major revival and renewal will take place!

Other Fasts

In addition to the seven (7) fasts, there are several others that may not be as common, but are certainly as effective!

The Ezra Fast: Fasting For Spiritual Breakthrough and Protection –Ezra 8: 21 – 23

By reading this Scripture you will see that Ezra called for a nationwide Fast to:

➢ Seek Him for guidance for them

➢ Seek Him for the youth

➢ Seek for Protection of their possessions

Ezra did not request soldiers and horsemen to help them against the enemy, He had spoken to the king about the God he served; He knew, as a servant of God, that the hand of God would be on those who are *for* God – who seek Him first according to Matthew 6: 33. Remember, He promised Guidance and Protection from the enemies.

The Lord also knows that His power and wrath are against those who forsake Him. (See II Chronicles 15: 2; Psalm 34: 12 – 16; Jeremiah 29: 11 – 14) But He will be with you if you seek Him.
Ezra 7: 24 says, *"Also we inform you that it shall not be lawful to impose tax, tribute or custom on any of the priests, Levites, singers, gatekeepers, Nethinim, or servants of this house of God."*

The Scripture clearly states that the House of God and His servant ought not to pay taxes.

The Priest Ezra, based on his God-given wisdom, set magistrates and judges. In addition, he was given instruction to teach those who did not know God's laws and statutes. (II Chronicles 17: 7; Ezra 7: 10; Malachi 2: 7 and Deuteronomy 16: 18 – 22)

Now, there are several further benefits as a result of this Ezra Fast including:

> Humility

> Guidance

> Protection

> Deliverance

> Assistance

This Fast is effective for the above. It shows that God is our security. No human security system can deliver us as God can. He will guard our substances.

Fasting involves a sacrificial denial of necessary nourishment, while turning one's attention to seeking God. During that denial, God wants you to give up something in order to get your breakthrough – meat, ice cream, coffee, beer, cigarettes, rice, sex – you must be willing to give up something that you love to get results.

You can also reduce your security costs by carrying out this fast, knowing the fact that your first protection comes from God!

Forty Day Fast

This Fast has numerous benefits

➢ Dominion

➢ Power

➢ Reversal of Judgement

Deuteronomy 9: 18 – 29 and Exodus 24: 18 reveal that as you do this Fast, the first out pouring of the Spirit of God will be upon you, and it will lift you out of the wilderness and all other places of struggle.

No food or water for 40 days – Jesus did this fast too Luke 4: 1 – 2. This Fast releases the Spirit so that you will walk in the supernatural.

The Fasts Of The Months

This comes from Zechariah 8: 18 – 19 which say:

"Then the word of the Lord of hosts came to me, saying, 'Thus says the Lord of hosts: The fast of the fourth month, the fast of the fifth, the fast of the seventh, the fast of the tenth, shall be joy and gladness and cheerful feasts for the house of Judah. Therefore love truth and peace.'"

There are several specific months throughout the course of the year that Fasting can be most effective!

The Fast of the Fourth Month – April (on our calendar). The number four (4) means "Reign and Rule over kingdoms and creation" according to Genesis 1; 16 & 18 – 19. Hence, these are the benefits that will be derived as a result of fasting during this month.

The Fast of the Fifth Month – May. The number five (5) means grace, the goodness of God, service, taxes, debt and sin according to Genesis 1: 20 – 23; Genesis 41: 34; Leviticus 21: 31. Please note that Egypt was not paying Tithes to the true and living God, and that was what caused the plague. Joseph realized that!

The Fast of the Seventh Month – July. The number seven (7) means *"complete, rest, finished, perfection"*. (Genesis 2: 1 & 3) This number also means *"debt cancellation"* Deuteronomy 15: 1 – 2. It will bring Spiritual blessings upon a nation!

The Fast of the Tenth Month – October. The number ten (10) means "test, tithe, temptation, trial. It also means "measure for purpose, accept or reject" Malachi 3: 10; Revelation 2: 10; Daniel 5: 27. God placed ten plagues upon Egypt as a judgement.

By obeying the word to call these fasts, individuals and nations will receive benefits such as is outlined in Zechariah 8: 18 – 19. National Fasts will transform into joyous feasts! If nations start to apply these principles, then God would bless mightily. The promises of God would be fulfilled upon nations and individuals.

All nations have a purpose to be accomplished on earth, and it is the duty of the leaders to find out from God what the purpose is for which their land was created. They must ask the following questions:

➢ *"Is this nation fulfilling its purpose according to God's plan?"*

➢ *"Are we giving God the opportunity to play His part in our nation-building?"*

What is the Prophetic Word for your nation? If God can use Egypt to help other nations (Genesis 41), then can't He use your nation to help other nations?

Once a nation applies Biblical Principles, then God will bless them so much that people from other nations will travel and visit that nation to:

➢ Trade

➢ Set up Businesses

➢ Invest in other areas of the country, and also

➢ Seek the source from which such wisdom comes – which is Jesus Christ.

Zechariah 7: 8 – 14 reveal that disobedience will result in captivity. So God is calling nations into repentance so that His blessings will come upon them.

Chapter 21

PRAYERS AND DECLARATIONS FOR THE NEW MILLIONAIRE

Here are several confessions that every new Millionaire must declare to receive and maintain victories.

The Billionaire Confession

In the name of Jesus Christ I **(insert your name here)** *declare that:*

I am a Billionaire!

I am full of Godly wisdom!

I am the most anointed to speak about wealth and Biblical Principles for generations to come!

I stand on Haggai 2: 8 – the silver is mine, the gold is mine says the Lord of Hosts. God has granted me II Chronicles 1: 12 which says:

"Wisdom and knowledge are granted to you; and I will give you riches and wealth and honor, such as none of the kings have had who were before you, nor shall any after you have the like."

The Lord will open to me His good treasure, the heavens to give the rain to my land in its seasons! God will bless all the work of my hands. I shall lend to many nations, but I shall not borrow!   Psalm 50: 10 – 11 says:

"For every beast of the forest is mine and the cattle on a thousand hills.   I know all the birds of the mountains, and the wild beasts of the field are Mine."

Lord, sell some of those to cash and assets and release it all to me now in Jesus' name!

As II Chronicles 9: 22 – 23 say, I (__insert your name here__) *surpassed all the kings of the earth in riches and wisdom. And all the kings of the earth will seek the presence of (your name here) for the Godly wisdom which God has put in my heart.*

II Chronicles 9: 13 – 14 declares that gifts shall come to me in abundance from Kings, Queens, businessmen, the poor, the fatherless, widows, the IRS, banks, merchants, traders and governors.   Weights of gold shall come to me yearly – six hundred and sixty-six talents!

According to verse 24, **"each man brought his present; articles of silver and gold, garments, armor, spices, horses, and mules at a set rate year by year"**.   **[NB. "... horses and mules..." were vehicles in those days; so for today, it refers to vehicles of all kinds – cars, buses, planes etc.]**

I declare that this blessing will take effect now in the name of Jesus!

I declare and receive the anointing, favor and grace from God to remain humble! AMEN!

Confession For Mistakes In Business

Father, in Jesus' name, I confess and release all mistakes that I have made in business relationships, the stock market, trading and with business partners. I confess and release all mistakes I have made by wrongly discerning business partners and motives; through mis-management, trusting the wrong persons, leaning to my own understanding, not seeking the Lord deeply before making decisions!

Right now, I release myself from all bad experiences in the past, in Jesus' name and I thank you Lord to bring forth new doors, new opportunities, new investments, new ideas, new friends, new wisdom and I thank you for the great future ahead!

I thank you that I am the new millionaire and that millions come to me from, the 7 continents. All my transactions from this day forth will turn into millions and billions!

I release all bitter memories, pride, offense and I thank you for victory in Jesus' name!

Amen!

Confession For Financial Deliverance

Almighty God, my heavenly Father, I come to you through Jesus Christ my Lord and Savior, and I DECREEE AND DECLARE that no weapon formed against me shall prosper, according to Isaiah 54: 17. Therefore:

I reject financial bondage

I reject lack and poverty

I reject recession and debt

Convert my debt to victory with blessings running over, fill up all my empty vessels, and let not the creditors have dominion over me. Perform that miracle as you did with the widow in II Kings 4: 1 – 7, who received an overflow. Convert this overflow into sales and Let the oil of blessing overflow for and in us, according to verse 6. According to Matthew 6: 12 forgive our debts as we forgive our debtors and do not lead us into temptation but deliver us from the evil one – especially creditors – for Yours is the Kingdom and the power and the glory forever!

I reject sin, sickness and, diseases, in Jesus' name

I reject the enemy's laughter at me in the name of Jesus.

Convert my mistakes to blessings in the name of Jesus and use me to attract money in Jesus' name. Let favor come from every direction in Jesus' name. Every nation will give into my life!

I declare that all my debt will be written off or paid in full, by unusual favor or by persons to whom You speak, in the name of Jesus! AMEN!

For more powerful prayers that will bring great victories to the life of the New Millionaire, they can be found in the book **Prayer Works!** © 2008

Chapter 22

EXCEL IN GIVING

II Corinthians 8

As you look into this Scripture, you realize that Paul was speaking to the Church at Corinth regarding giving to smaller churches.

There are many rich churches that have millions of dollars in Savings Accounts, Real Estate holdings, CD's, Bonds and other assets dormant; and have millions of dollars' worth of equipment stored up and rusting. They could give help to the poorer churches. Paul challenged the Corinthian Church regarding the Grace of Giving.

II Corinthians 8: 7 reveals that while the Corinthians had shown such zeal (See also I Corinthians 1: 4 – 7) and were enriched in everything – in faith, knowledge, utterance, diligence, spiritual gifts and lacked nothing tangible – they lacked grace in giving. They were rich in the realms of Spiritual Giftings and Finances and the grace of God was in their past, present and future. Paul was saying that as they abound in all grace, they must abound in the grace of giving.

Giving is an act of love, according to I John 3: 16 – 19, and James 2: 15 – 16; not only to those closest to you, but to your brothers and sisters in need, who have a work to accomplish or a God-given vision to bring forth! There are many right now, who are more than able to help financially, but are unwilling to do so. Is the love of God in them?

Love is shown not only in heroic deeds of self-sacrifice, but in a daily life of compassion.

II Corinthians 8: 8 lets us know that the gift being given must be voluntary. II Corinthians 9: 5 – 7 says:

"Therefore I thought it necessary to exhort the brethren to go to you ahead of time, and prepare your generous gift beforehand, which you had previously promised, that it may be ready as a matter of generosity and not as a grudging obligation. But this I say: He who sows sparingly will also reap sparingly and he who sows bountifully will also reap bountifully. So let each one give as he purposes in his heart, not grudgingly or of necessity, for God loves a cheerful giver."

The greatest and most inspiring example of generosity is the grace of Jesus!
In Ephesians 4:4, Spiritual unity is the key to spiritual warfare. It is unity in the spirit. This was so much a part of life and teaching of the early Church. Causing division among God's people was a very serious matter in the early church as it ought to be today. Paul instructs on this matter in Titus 3: 9 – 11.

Acts 4: 32 – 33 speak of the people being of one heart, one soul. None among them said anything of the things they possessed was his, but they had all things in common.

Acts 4: 33 says:

"And with great power the apostles gave witness to the resurrection of the Lord Jesus. And great grace was upon them all"

"And with great power..." means with great strength, especially physical strength. It speaks of Dominion, Authority, energy, might great force, great ability, and dramatic transformation. This is the norm for the Spirit-filled church!

Spiritual Unity

According to the Scripture, they were breathing spiritually together; they shared everything and they had all things in common. They witnessed with great power and great grace was upon them all – Acts 4: 23 – 31 – one accord, one voice together.

The moment the Church begins to walk in one heart and soul – one accord – then revival *will* come. The Church must share together having one thing in common. God is not pleased with those who call on His name while trying to bring division in the Body, preaching segregation in the Body. The sinners are more united in what they do than the Church.

If it is *"one Lord, one Faith, one Baptism, one God and one Father of all, who is above all and in you all..."* then why can't people be of one heart, one soul, sharing in all things?

One Accord

Philippians 2: 1 – 2 speaks of 'one accord', which speaks to being of the same mind, having the same love and spiritual unity. So do John 17: 20 – 23, Acts 2: 42 – 47; Ephesians 4: 3 – 6; I Peter 3: 8; and II Chronicles 30: 12.

The Holy Spirit is a source of unity. He brings us together in oneness. (Galatians 3: 28) Some persons are more interested in being in unity with their denomination, rather than the ministry of the Holy Spirit

Blockages – racial, cultural or social differences, education levels, positions, financial status, political beliefs, stand between Christians. Christ must be first and foremost and you must set aside the secondary things. (I Corinthians 13: 1 – 13; Philippians 4: 1 – 6)

The Holy Spirit is the only one that can cause singleness of heart, which will result in obedience to kings and leaders.

Psalm 133: 1 speaks also of Unity. It helps you to recognize that for nations to get that type of intervention from God they must first obey God's instructions. They must allow God to be the center and first of all. Then, He will bring unity. No man can bring unity; God works on man's heart to bring unity!

An Opportunity To Be Blessed

Now investing in the Kingdom of God is the greatest opportunity that you have to be a blessing and to be blessed. When you are given the opportunity to give and to invest in the House of God and into the lives of the men and women of God, don't be like others who give excuses like:

'I'm already giving to charity.'

Proverbs 19: 17 says, *"He who has pity on the poor lends to the Lord, and He will pay back what he has given."*

Or some say,

'I'll have to pray about it.'

But throughout the entire Holy Bible the Lord already admonishes you and gives you the go ahead to give. Remember, you will never lose anything by giving to the House of God and to the man and woman of God.
But when you sow into the Kingdom of God, that is a lifetime investment, that God will never forget. A seed can change the heart of God, according to Genesis 8: 20 - 22, when God said that He would never again curse the ground.

In Genesis 9, God blessed Noah and his family because of the seed he sowed. It may not be a financial blessing, but your family will be protected and you will have peace and good health.

Now look at the benefits in Luke 7: 1 – 10 given to those who build the Kingdom.

The centurion's servant was sick and ready to die. The centurion sent the elders of the Jews to Jesus asking Him to come and heal his servant. As the came before the Lord Jesus, they told Him of the things the centurion had done for God's people and His House. They said he:

➢   Loved the nation

➢   Built them a synagogue

Because of that, his servant was delivered from death and God raised him up because he invested in the people of God and in the House of God.

God will be quicker to heal the sick that have sown into the Kingdom of God. (See also Acts 9: 36 – 42)

A person who refuses to sow when God speaks will forfeit his/her harvest and God will give that harvest to someone else who is faithful. Just remember, when God tells you to give, it is because He has a harvest in mind that He wants to release to you.

How To Be Blessed To Receive Promotion

Matthew 10: 30 – 42 and Mark 9: 41 tell you that those who give support to the messengers of the Lord will receive blessings.

By receiving the Lord's representatives -   Apostles, Prophets, Evangelists, Pastors Teachers and the man or woman that serves God - you are receiving Him! God's representatives can unlock any blessing in your life, including healing and deliverance.

Elijah And The Widow

I Kings 17: 8 – 16 speak of a widow who was nearly without foodstuff and was asked to give her last to the Prophet of God, Elijah. She was told that if she did, God would give her an unfailing provision. This woman overcame the fear and responded in faith, and God was faithful to His promise. Her obedience relieved her from famine, financial problems, debt and release of a major blessing – the miracle for her son.

Remember this, blessings come to you, but you may turn it away through your disobedience!

In II Kings 4: 1 – 7, it is seen that the prophet Elisha had the anointing to take the widow out of debt, while leaving more than enough for him on which to live. The anointing on the Prophets' lives unlocks the miracle you desire.

In II Kings 4: 8 – 37, the Shunnamite woman was wealthy but wise. Look at the miracle she received by feeding the man of God! Further to this, she made a small upper room, and that seed resurrected the vision that seemed dead – she conceived a child. Her seed continued to bear fruit as she gave to the prophet

The prophetic presence will stop every attack against you and resurrect every dead thing.

Mary Magdalene

Look at Mary's life outlined in Luke 8: 1 – 3 and John 12: 1 - 8. She sowed into Jesus' ministry. She also sowed expensive spikenard as she used it to anoint Jesus' feet. Its value was three hundred (300) denarii. One (1) denarius was a day's wages, so this was the equivalent of approximately 10 months' wages. While others were confused about her actions, it was clear that she understood servant-hood. As a result, she was the first to see the risen Lord! (Mark 16: 1 – 10; John 20: 1 – 18)

In Luke 10: 38 – 42, Martha had a legitimate concern. She wanted to ensure that she was a proper hostess. But Mary's concern was to be a proper disciple – to hear His word, do it and support Jesus' ministry. That is what is needed!

Look at what happened in Acts 2: 44 – 47; Acts 4: 32 – 37, and as you read, realize that there was no lack!

Elisha And Elijah

II Kings 2: 1 – 17 show you that for Elisha to receive the impartation from Elijah, he had to stay with him and serve. It is this servant-hood that allowed Elisha to receive the double portion of the anointing for his ministry. The term 'serve' here means he:

➢   Gave to the man of God

➢   Lifted up the hand of the man of God (Carried out whatever was necessary to ensure that the man of God could accomplish his task.

➢   Stood in the gap for the man of God

> ➤ Followed the man of God to Bethel, Jericho, Jordan and wherever he went

The mantle was a symbol of authority that will enable you to perform miracles.

It is important to recognize a few things.

> ➤ Curses can cause famine II Samuel 21. Get back to the foundation and deal with the sins of the former leaders or administration. Repentance, restitution, seed and sin offering and God will heed the prayers of the land. II Samuel 24: 25 speaks of the plagues.

> ➤ Always seek for an opportunity to give; this will release promotion/rewards to you that will take you out of debt and increase your salary/income. (I Chronicles 10: 6) I Samuel 17: 25 speaks of the rewards to solve problems and bring promotion.

The Mighty Men Of David

I Chronicles 11: 10 tells you that these men knew how to serve – they made David their king. They strengthened themselves with him and they were faithful to the leader. They put their lives on the line for their leaders! (I Chronicles 11: 17 – 20) Three (3) took on three hundred (300).

According to Luke 5, because the fisherman lent Jesus their boat to carry out the gospel, their obedience created a miracle that was not usual. The Fishermen knew that the best time to catch fish was at night. They were struggling to catch all night. But by obeying Jesus, He released to them the prophetic instruction to launch out into the deep. Luke 5: 6 – 7, they caught so much that their nets were breaking; they had to signal to their partners and others in the industry to help them harness this catch! Their seed changed their lives and they were able to move from one profession to the next. They could survive from that catch for a long time; their business partners could just work while they worked for God.

As you read Exodus 36: 1 – 7, you see that the children of Israel brought freewill offering every morning, to build the sanctuary. Moses had to eventually restrain the people from giving, because they were bringing in more than enough to build. God is calling back His people to bring in the freewill offering so that they will be blessed.

They can also bring in, according to Exodus 35: 22, jewelry of gold earrings, nose rings, rings and necklaces as an offering to build!

Chapter 23

THE POWER OF A SEED

In Christendom, a seed is regarded as anything given whether to a Church/ministry or to a person, particularly but not only, to a man or woman of God to be a blessing or to meet a need. What is given takes on the characteristics of a natural seed and germinates and grows and brings a harvest to both giver and recipient. Solomon understood the Seed Principle and that is why he was so wise – it was a seed that caused him to receive great wisdom. Realize that generally, a seed opens doors and gives access. Further to this, a seed:

- ➤ Stops plagues and brings reformation to a nation – II Chronicles 15: 11

- ➤ Brings the prophetic word to fulfillment in your life – Genesis 15

- ➤ Brings Healing – Genesis 20: 14 - 20

- ➤ Gives you great wisdom, according to II Chronicles 1

- ➤ Releases to you knowledge, riches and wealth, according to II Chronicles 1: 12

- ➤ Brings great people in your midst to finance your vision – II Chronicles 9: 9

- ➤ Brings peace in to a nation – II Chronicles 15: 3 – 8

➤ Allows you to be able to enter into a covenant with God, because according to II Chronicles 15: 12, you cannot enter into a covenant with God without a seed

➤ Opens the heavens to release new business ideas – II Chronicles 1: 13 – 17

➤ Stops the enemies (even during a famine) and cause wells to open up – Genesis 26; Malachi 2: 19

➤ Breaks curses, including generational and financial curses – Genesis 8: 20 – 22

➤ Brings deliverance and stops the flood – Genesis 8: 1 – 5

➤ Changes the heart of God – Genesis 8: 21 – 22
➤ Brings blessing, increase and fruit for you and your family – Genesis 9: 1 (NB '9' means '*harvest, fruit, fruitfulness, fruition*')

➤ Always allows God to remember His covenant with you – Genesis 9: 13 – 17

➤ Brings you and your prayers as a memorial before God and therefore brings you favor – Act 10: 1 – 4

➤ Can give you 100-fold return if sown in good soil – Genesis 26: 12

➤ In conjunction with obedience brings a 3-dimensional blessing according to Genesis 26: 12 – 13, so you:

- Begin to prosper
- Continue prospering
- Be very prosperous

➤ Allow your enemy to fear you and leave you – Genesis 26: 16

➤ Allow you to find hidden treasures and wells – Genesis 26: 19

➤ Let God appear to you and bless you – Genesis 26: 24

➤ Allows you to receive your father's blessing. This is also the inheritance seed – Genesis 27

NB Genesis is the 1st Book and it speaks of the inheritance in Chapter 27. Hence the Inheritance Seed is 127 i.e. $127.

1 - Creation, first, rank, order

2 - Divide, judge, separate, discern

7 - Complete, finish, rest

The Inheritance Seed releases to you your father's inheritance quickly.

Interestingly, Genesis 27: 27 – 29 reveal that your spiritual or natural father's blessing releases to you three (3) types of blessings:

➢   Material Prosperity

➢   Political Supremacy

➢   Cursing on all your enemies

Recognize that anything which opposes God, your future, your God-given vision, your prosperity, and generally anything that wants to stop you is your enemy. This seed will cause you to get that spiritual or natural blessing of which the enemy wants to rob you. As a result and according to the word of God in Genesis 12: 3, God will:

"...bless those who bless you and ... curse him who curses you..."

Other Reasons For Seed-Sowing

There are further reasons you must sow seed. For instance,

➢   To get revelation knowledge – Genesis 15: 7 – 20

➢   To receive your desire, along with wisdom and knowledge from God's servant – II Chronicles 9: 9 – 12

> ➢ Sowing your firstfruits and paying your Tithes will bring you great blessings – II Chronicles 31: 5 – 10

Additionally, you must recognize that according to I Chronicles 21: 18, a good seed stops plagues and restrains judgement.

Leadership Ranks For Giving

Nation Leaders

II Chronicles 24: 12 – 14 clearly reveal that Kings, Queens, Prime Ministers and Presidents must sow seed (give money & resources) for the repair of the temple so that the nation will be blessed. Further to this, II Chronicles 35: 7 – 8 encourage leaders to sow seed during the Passover to the priests totaling 30,000 units and an additional 3,000 units from their personal possessions. Today, that could be $30,000 and an additional $3,000 from their personal possessions.

The number '30' means *'acceptable, conform, mature'*. It means coming into a level of maturity which requires us to conform to the image of God that you may ultimately be acceptable to Him and in His sight. (Romans 8: 29, Numbers 4: 3) Hence, once there is conformation, then one has come into maturity and acceptability.

Scripturally, a person could not begin serving in the temple (start their ministry) until he was thirty (30) years of age. Jesus and Joseph serve as prime examples, according to Numbers 4: 3, Luke 3: 23, Genesis 41: 46, and Psalm 105: 19.

According to II Samuel 5: 4, David was also thirty (30) years of age, when He was promoted.

It is noteworthy that the number '3' means *'conform, obey, imitate and trinity'* as Genesis 1: 9, 11 and 13 reveal.

By sowing the $30,000 seed, the king was conforming, obeying in order to be prosperous. Remember that all numbers mean something Biblically /Scripturally.

The Leaders Under The Nation Leaders

In II Chronicles 35: 8 it shows that the king's leaders would give to the priest and his administration during the Passover two thousand six hundred units ($2600)

2000   -   Mature judgement (good judgement)

600   -   Image of man

The king's leaders followed the good example set by their leader – the king – which showed mature/good judgement. Joshua 3: 4 tells you that Joshua instructed that there be a space between them and their leaders, and that they follow.

Relatives Of The King

II Chronicles 35: 9 states that the brother of a king, queen, Prime Minister or President must give five thousand (5000) units ($5000). Note that the number '5' means *'grace, mature service, life'.* (See also Leviticus 27: 31 and Genesis 41: 34)

Sowing the Passover seed is a must for all leaders, and individuals who want to be successful in life. God must be obeyed at all costs; and once that is done, it will bring great blessing.

A Word On The Harvest

You can look at a rich man and identify the area of lack in his life – this tells us that there is lack in other areas of his life. Understand therefore that:

➢ The gift of giving is a gift from God

➢ Wealth is a blessing from God. Job's wealth was a result of God's blessing. Abraham's blessing is God's wealth released!

With all that has been said thus far, the question at this juncture is, *'How does someone determine how and where to sow?'*

Here's how:

➢ Obey God's voice – Deuteronomy 28: 1

> ➢ Sow where the Lord instructs – Deuteronomy 12

> ➢ Accept that God is the one who gives the increase and not man - I Corinthians 3: 6

You must recognize that people will always be attracted to, and want to give based on the earthly status of man and not God's instructions. However, you must also know that giving based on God's instructions will carry the greatest harvest.

Many in the Body of Christ have not and cannot fully receive their harvest, because they are not listening to and obeying God's instructions to them on where and even when to sow. Instead they ignore the local church and give to large ministries and churches believing that there is a greater blessing there because of its size.

All is not lost however, because God is now raising up financial prophets to bring back the wealth to the local church, and not just in one area!

You must recognize and accept several underlying principles of the Kingdom of God:

> ➢ The Kingdom of God operates similar to the system of the tree. If you don't plant a seed to bring a tree there will be no harvest. (Matthew 7: 17 – 20)

> ➢ God's system is the original banking system. When you deposit, you will receive returns with interest added to it. (Matthew 25: 14; Luke 19)

The principles of God and His Kingdom always guarantee return and blessing as you sow.

The Power Of Giving And Sowing Seed

According to II King 4: 8, giving and sowing seed:

- ➢ Opens wombs to conceive a vision or a son

- ➢ Breaks barrenness

- ➢ Restores old things to life and gives them stamina and vitality

- ➢ Opens the door for a prophetic blessing on your life, and

- ➢ A seed can give you a miracle between 7 – 9 months, for things that seem impossible; the period for the time of delivery, whether it is a child or a vision

- ➢ By feeding the man of God, building an upper room, it will bring great prosperity to your family.

- ➢ It brings a blessing that looks like a curse and it breaks the curse of not conceiving and brings the blessing.

In those days it was customary – though not sanctioned by God for a man to take a second wife, when his first was barren. Any woman who could not bear a child was viewed as a curse.

I Samuel 1: 3 – 5 states that you will see that Elkanah would obey the laws by appearing before God as stated in Deuteronomy 12: 5 – 7. He would go to receive the blessing by taking His tithes and offering which is seed. (Deuteronomy16: 6)

In Luke 2: 41 – 42 you see Jesus' parents walking in obedience by attending the Feasts every year according to the custom, to receive the blessing.

Now by reading this, you realize that each time it came to giving offerings, Hannah's husband would give a double portion. The double portion:

➢ Creates the miracle

➢ Shuts up all your opposition and rivals

➢ Silences the enemies so you can smile at them

➢ Opens the womb

Additionally, according to I Samuel 1: 21, the husband leads the charge in this Scripture. On the other hand, the wife in II Kings 4: 8 took charge in order that her household would receive the blessing.

Chapter 24

BIBLICAL FACTS ABOUT THE SEED

The word of God in Ecclesiastes 11: 6 says:

"In the morning sow your seed; and in the evening do not withhold your hand; for you do not know which will prosper, either this or that, or whether both alike will be good."

As has already established, the seed includes money, the word of God, love, prayers of intercession and anything that can be given to be used as a tool to create your future. The Scripture reminds you to keep sowing because you never know what will prosper. Just sow and let it grow according to Ecclesiastes 11: 3 – 4.

Discerning market conditions with natural human knowledge will not help us. All businesses must be spiritually discerned because God is the One Who makes all things. Whoever attempts to properly discern by what they see naturally will not walk in prosperity. You cannot discern by natural market conditions. Ecclesiastes 11: 4 tells us that the natural wind is not what you should observe.

Ecclesiastes 11: 5 further tells you that the Spiritual Wind, which is the Holy Spirit, is what you must observe, particularly in business. John 3: 8 declares that in order to understand the wind, you must be born again.

Sowing For Daily Provision

Sowing seed is an imperative and compulsory principle done for various reasons from a Biblical standpoint. There are many things for which you can sow seed, and one such thing is **Daily Provision**. Exodus 16 speaks of sowing for Daily Provision. So you can, for example, sow **$16** based on Exodus 16 for your Daily Provision. Additionally, you can sow a seed of **$11.03** from Luke 11: 3 for bread from heaven – your Daily Provision.

It is interesting to note that this seed for Daily Provision will allow God to give you a double portion so that you will not have to toil on the Sabbath or Sunday – the day of worship. God does not want His people to toil on the day of worship, and that is why He gives a double portion. You can sow this seed and ask the Lord to let His glory be revealed in your finances

God wants His people to:

- ➢ Rest from poverty
- ➢ Rest on His day of worship instead of working to pay bills

- ➢ Sow, that seed can be produced for sowing on a daily basis.

The number '16' means *'without boundaries, without limitations, free-spirited, without law and without sin'*, according to Romans 4: 15 and Acts 27: 34, 37 – 38.

'Manna', was the Hebrew name given by the Israelites to the bread that came from heaven daily. The term means

'what is it', and it had the flavor of coriander, a seed-producing herb that grows 2 – 3 feet tall.

In addition to the Daily Provision seed, a small seed of $6.13 from Matthew 6: 13 can be sown for the following:

➤ Protection from temptations

➤ Protection from the evil ones (their plans and schemes)

➤ The manifestation of the power and glory of God forever, for kingdom purpose

Remember, a small seed can produce major harvest.

Bread And Wealth

Those who are wealthy must live by the Word of God if they expect to maintain their wealth. There are several simple keys for the wealthy based on Deuteronomy 8: 3 with regard to this matter.

➤ Man cannot live by bread alone, but by every word that proceeds from the mouth of the Lord

➤ Natural bread cannot nourish the soul

➤ There cannot be survival of the soul without God's Word daily bread, the manna, which was previously explained.

➢ The prayer found in Matthew 6: (especially vs 11) was encouraged by Jesus. Without daily bread, the physical needs cannot be dealt with, including:

- Forgiveness of sins
- Revelation for debt cancellation
- Revelation for breakthrough

The word, according to I Peter 2:2, allows you to grow; you cannot grow without the Word – certainly not spiritually! Remember this:

➢ Every word that proceeds from the mouth of God is life

➢ Every word that proceeds from the mouth of God always brings a solution to your problems

Man cannot survive without God's word; so to be too busy for God and His word will lead to mounting problems.

Interestingly, men study how to make millions, but many do not study the word of God which tells them how to live and maintain the millions they make. They don't study:

- How to be a good steward
- How to put God first
- How to be rich and have peace
- How the Lord gives riches

and it can all be found in Deuteronomy 8: 1 -2

Now, as you read and understand the word of God, you will realize and know that your original and basic source of life is God. You will also recognize that great wealth, magnificent real estate, increase in assets, businesses, stocks that perform well, liquid assets, gold, silver – everything in which you have prospered (Deuteronomy 8: 12 – 14) must be attributed to God. You must not forget the Lord who gives the increase. Take note that:

> ➢ When you read the Word you will realize that you must not touch God's glory and say that it is your power and your hand that has caused you to gain your wealth. (Deuteronomy 8: 17)

> ➢ When you read the Word you will remember that it is God who gives you the power to get wealth. (Deuteronomy 8: 18)

> ➢ When you read the Word you will realize that your wealth is for the purpose of establishing His covenant. (Deuteronomy 8: 18) Therefore, you must Tithe, sow seed, build the Church according to Malachi 3: 10, Genesis 8: 22 and Haggai 1, that His covenant be established for and through you.

Do not use your wealth to follow other gods, which are not the true and living God. Serving and worshipping them only lead to destruction, not only of you and your family and business, but also the nation.

God does not want us to be hungry for the natural bread, the natural things of the world only but also for the Word of God, according to Luke 4: 4. If you are not hungry for the things of God, this will cause you to give

257

up your rights and blessings, and worship the devil and the things of the world, according to Luke 4: 5 – 8.

Barrenness And Birth

The term *'barrenness'* carries several meanings from spiritual and natural perspectives. It is therefore important to understand the term and all it entails.

'Barrenness' is:

> ➤ The state of being unfruitful and unable to produce or reproduce

> ➤ Being without the facilities, resources to perform or to yield a harvest from one's efforts, seed or deposits; empty; void of power, strength or energy

Barrenness is the absence of fruitfulness on one's effort or the inability to produce profitable fruit. It can stem from generational curses, or it can be a curse released by God (Deuteronomy 7: 13 – 15). It can also come from the enemy.

There are several women in the Bible that were barren but the Lord overturned their barrenness to fulfill His promise through prophecy. In all instances, the Lord's word was sent forth to overturn the conditions and eliminate the barriers that were preventing pregnancy – spiritual or natural.

Out of barrenness great things are birthed!

> ➤ Hannah gave birth to Samuel – I Samuel 1: 20

> ➤ Sarah gave birth to Isaac – Genesis 21: 1 - 7

> ➤ The Shunammite woman gave birth to a son - II Kings 4: 8

II Kings 2: 21 speaks of the barren place. The prophet used salt and broke the barrenness. As a result:

> ➤ The land became fruitful

> ➤ The house became fruitful

> ➤ Businesses became fruitful

> ➤ Churches become fruitful

To break barrenness you must employ the following tools:

> ➤ Prayer & Fasting

> ➤ Seed-sowing

> ➤ Crying out to the Lord God

> ➤ Obedience

Barrenness is a kind of famine also, as in I Kings 17. Note the instruction of the Lord that was given to the widow in verse 10:

"... 'Please bring me a little water in a cup, that I may drink.' And as she was going to get it, he called to her and said, 'Please bring me a morsel of bread in your hand."

As you read the story of the widow and Elijah, recognize that as a result of her obedience to the instruction, her famine broke and her son was restored to life.

Chapter 25

BLESSING LEADERSHIP THROUGH SEED

Psalm 72 & I Kings 2

Psalm 72 was dedicated to the Prosperity of Solomon, at the beginning of his reign. I Kings 2 is David's instructions to the leader:

➢ Be strong and prove yourself a man

➢ Keep the change of the Lord, your God

➢ Walk in His ways, keep His statutes and commandments, judgements, and His testimony

This will bring prosperity in all that you do and wherever you turn. That all the promises spoken by the Lord for you will come to pass – prophetic – dreams and visions

All the Godly leaders would give a change/blessing that those who are going to take over the mantle would obey the change that will lead to prosperity. God desires that all His leaders walk in prosperity according to I Kings 2: 4. It asks us to

➢ Walk in truth before God

➢ Love God with all your heart and with all your souls, then the linage would continue

The leader would also instruct the new Leader/Administration who will watch whom and to whom they will show kindness, who to judge and remove from the Administration when they take over – as in I Kings 2: 5 – 8.

By reading the old covenant, it may not be a king obedient to the law of Moses anymore; but a king obedient to Biblical Principles and to Jesus' instruction if they want to be prosperous – as in I Corinthians – naturally and spiritually.

In I Kings 2: 5, David outlines to Solomon the conduct of the Chief of the military, things he had done after the warfare ended - II Samuel 3: 27. This brought his punishment as a murderer – according to II Samuel 20: 10.

David clearly outlined to Solomon that he should deal with the people he (David) neglected to deal with. If you have persons that are murderers, or are in the security forces and have not been brought to justice, know that it can affect an Administration. (II Kings 2: 31)

A wise king sometimes has to put measures in place to deal with rival factors; and other uprising affecting an Administration; this so that the Administration will move with peace.

There are some persons in organizations that you have to keep under close watch, as is seen in I Kings 2: 36.

The Solomonic Seeds

Solomon's wisdom is known by many through the ages to date; and there are seeds that can be sown to receive some of the Godly wisdom he had. Take note of these three (3) points:

> Psalm 72 was dedicated to the prosperity of Solomon - $72 Seed

> The number '7' means *'complete; all finished; rest'* (Genesis 1, 6 & 8)

> The number '2' means *'divide; judge; separate; discern'*

Sowing this seed from the Word will give the following blessings:

> A Just Reign   72: 1 – 4

> A Universal Reign   72: 5 – 11

> A Compassionate Reign   72: 12 – 14

> A Prosperous Reign   72: 15 – 17

> A Glorious Reign   72: 18 – 20

As you water the seed with prayer, then the king will faithfully discharge God's justice on the nations.

When a king or a leader rules well, with justice and compassion, the earth itself will react:

➤ There will be peace in the nation.

➤ The mountains and hills will yield their fruits

➤ Hidden Treasures will be revealed

➤ Great prosperity will come upon individuals and the nation

➤ There will be expansion of territory

➤ Kings and Leaders from different nations shall sow into your ministry as they did with Solomon's Administration. Psalm 72: 15, for example, speaks of how Sheba served Solomon with their wealth.

Psalm 72: 16 speaks of abundance of grain in the earth (prosperity) for those in the city. Verse 17 speaks of blessing from all nations' children's children shall be blessed. In Genesis 12: 12, God will bless all those who will bless you and will curse those who will curse you.

Whoever curses God's authority, God will always return vengeance on them according to I Kings 2: 5 – 8. There are some things you need to realize:

➤ God wants His people to know that all blessings are from God (Psalm 1)

➤ You must not take God's blessings lightly (Psalm 23)

➢ When you are prospering, don't think it is your intellect or your academic qualifications, recognize that it is God

➢ When God blesses you, everything becomes easier, favor will fall in place, money will fall into place and wisdom will fall in place!

➢ Every success in life is because of the blessings of God

➢ The blessings of the Lord, through our lives will bring the whole earth, will be filled with His glory according to Nehemiah 9: 5 and Hebrews 2: 14

Chapter 26

NEW SEEDS FOR TRUE PROSPERITY

Here are some important Seeds you will need to sow as New Millionaires that will cause you not only to receive true wealth, but also to maintain it.

Scripture	Explanation	Amount
Isaiah 50: 4 – 9	This seed is powerful. ➢ It will give you the tongue of the learned and they will marvel about how you speak (John 7: 46) ➢ You will always know how to speak a word in Season to him who is weary ➢ God will open your sight and your hearing each morning to hear as the learned ➢ Your ears will open to a higher level ➢ God will always help you and no disgrace will come upon you ➢ You will triumph in all legal battles, spiritually or naturally	$50, $50,000

Scripture	Explanation	Amount
Isaiah 50: 10 - 11	All God's wealth belongs to His people; and in order to get God's wealth, you will need to sow for it. He says that the cattle on a thousand hills belong to Him. Birds of the mountains and the wild beasts of the field are His. The number '50' relates to ministry, just as '30' does according to Numbers 4: 23. As discussed earlier, '30' deals with the ministers' character. However, '50' deals with *service*. Solomon had five hundred and fifty (550) leaders over his work force, according to I Kings 9: 23. Luke 9: 14 tells us that Jesus instructed His disciples to allow the people He was feeding to sit in groups of fifties. The number fifty (50) also refers to '*jubilee*'. In addition to this, Pentecost was fifty (50) days after the Passover.	**$50, $50,000**

Scripture	Explanation	Amount
Psalm 46	➤ According to Genesis 1: 14 – 19, the number four '4' means *'reigns/rules (heaven and earth), light (day/night), signs and seasons'*. It also means *'resurrection'* according to John 11. ➤ The number '6', according to Genesis 1: 24 – 31 and Revelation 13: 18, represents *'man, image, dominion, subdue, meat (provision), labor, fruit/fruitful, multiply, prosperity, finance and souls'*. ➤ The number '40' means *'dominion, rule, acceptable or unacceptable'*. Having identified the benefits of the number '46' here are some others that come from Psalm 46: ➤ He is always present ➤ He gives strength ➤ He gives shelter, coverage and protection ➤ He cleanses and gives peace, refuge, life, anointing and security	**$46**

Scripture	Explanation	Amount
Amos 9: 13	➢ By sowing this seed you will be reaping so quickly, the blessing will be so great that it will be so difficult to finish one cycle before the next cycle begins. ➢ This seed will also bring stability, security, restoration for the things that were lost. ➢ The number '9' means *'harvest, trust, truthfulness, fruition'* according to Luke 17: 17 and Hebrews 13: 15 ➢ This blessing is for those who sow seed, for as verse 13 says: *"'Behold the days are coming', says the Lord, 'when the plowman shall overtake the reaper, and the treader of grapes him who sows seed; the mountains shall drip with sweet wine, and all the hills shall flow with it.'"* So the blessings will overtake those who sow seed. This is the time and season when God will, according to verse 11, • Restore the tabernacle • Repair its damages • Rebuild the ruins as in the days of old that the Glory of God may manifest in every area of our lives. ➢ It is noteworthy that the demonstration of the Kingdom power in all areas of the nation will also come, particularly in the areas of finance and politics	**$9.13, $913, $913,000**

Scripture	Explanation	Amount
Amos 9: 13 (cont'd)	*Noteworthy* Take note and understand that only those who are willing to sow toward the building of the Kingdom will experience the glory, wealth, power, favor of God in the last days. God's people shall no longer be the minority. They shall be landowners. They shall dominate in the end time. God's people shall benefit from their labor. They will not labor in vain! Pray more! The very waste cities they build, they shall inhabit them. Many of God's people have built or produced top of the line products but cannot dwell in or own them. It is going to change. They will build them and live in them (own them). All God wants is that His people remain faithful in sowing to build the Kingdom. This Promise must be fulfilled because this is part of the possession of land He promised to Abraham and his descendants – and you are his descendants!	$9.13, $913, $913,000

Scripture	Explanation	Amount
I Kings 17	➢ For the anointing to warn kings of drought and impending danger ahead, in addition to God's favor and grace. ➢ That God will provide a rich widow to feed us in the time of famine ➢ That you will receive more solutions for the economic situation	$17, $1700, $17,000
Deuteronomy 28: 14	➢ This seed is sown so that God may release His promised blessing upon you, according to His word, for your obedience.	$28, $28.14, $2,814, $28,014
Psalm 31: 20	This seed protects you from: • The plots of man • The strife of tongues You must realize that the tongue can cause damage to us, especially words spoken by those in authority. From time to time, people will speak against you, your property, which will result in your struggle and hardship. The tongue is a weapon, as is found in James 3: 6. Here the tongue: • Is a Fire • Is a world of Iniquity • Can defile the whole body The true source of the unruly evil produced by the tongue is hell. The tongue spits deadly poison and is manipulated by wicked spirits	$31.20, $3,120, $31,020

Scripture	Explanation	Amount
Isaiah 54: 17	➤ This seed protects you from evil plots, accusations, the tongue; God will foil all evil plots and condemn all tongues against you.	**54.17, $5,417, $54,017**
Jeremiah 5: 14	➤ This seed is for the Fire Anointing – which is for God to touch your tongue so that His word will come with fire	**$5.14, $514, $5.01**
Isaiah 61	This seed is for ministry. However, an individual can also sow this seed for his/her family that God will bless and use them. It is so that: ➤ The anointing for healing will come upon the leaders and the ministry ➤ God will use the ministry to proclaim liberty to the captives ➤ The ministry will proclaim the acceptable year of the Lord ➤ The ministry shall be called the tree of righteousness ➤ The ministry shall rebuild the old ruins and raise up the former desolations ➤ God will use the ministry to comfort those that mourn ➤ God will give the leaders and members beauty for ashes and the oil of joy for mourning and the spirit of praise for heaviness	**$61, $61,000**

Scripture	Explanation	Amount
Isaiah 61 (cont'd)	➤ The ministry, its leaders and members shall eat the riches of the Gentiles and in their glory shall the leaders and members boast ➤ Instead of shame the leaders and members of the ministry shall get double honor ➤ Instead of confusion, there will be rejoicing in the land and double and everlasting joy shall belong to the ministry, its leaders and members ➤ The ministry's descendants shall be known among the Gentiles and its offspring shall be known among the people and whoever sees them shall acknowledge them ➤ Strangers shall stand and feed the flock of the ministry ➤ The sons of foreigners shall be plowmen and vinedressers to the ministry, its leaders and its members; the leaders and members shall be known as the priests of the Lord and they shall be called the servants of God ➤ The Lord shall cause righteousness and praise to spring forth from the ministry before all nations ➤ The ministry, its leaders and members are the posterity whom the Lord has blessed	$61, $61,000

Scripture	Explanation	Amount
Job 5: 21	➤ This seed seals the promise that you will be hidden from the scourge of tongues and you shall not be afraid of destruction when it comes. Sow this seed to tame the tongue	$5.21, $521
Job 5: 15	This seed saves the needy: ➤ From the sword/destruction ➤ From the mouth of the mighty ➤ From their hands	$5.15, $515
Job 5: 19	This seed is: ➤ For deliverance from trouble ➤ That no one shall touch you	$5.19, $519
Job 5: 20	This seed is for ➤ Deliverance in the famine ➤ Deliverance in war and from death	$5.20, $520
Job 5: 22	This seed is sown that: ➤ You can laugh at destruction and famine ➤ You will not be afraid of the beast of the earth	$5.22, $522
Job 42:12	This seed is for : ➤ The restoration of wealth from God ➤ Prosperity	$42.12, $4,212
Exodus 23: 23	This seed is: ➤ For the conquest, that God will send angels to go before to cut off the enemy ➤ That you can possess the land and their wealth ➤ The removal of the obstacles (the 6 demons)	$23.23, $2,323

Scripture	Explanation	Amount
Revelation 5: 12	➤ This seed is for God to release the seven (7) blessings from above and to give you the seven benefits including rest from your enemies.	$512
Isaiah 26: 2 (Read 1 - 4)	➤ This is the immigration seed that God will open up the borders and gates and release favor to dwell in the land. ➤ It is also for Peace, salvation, health, happiness, creativity	$262
Psalm 147: 14	➤ The seed for Peace and Prosperity	$147.14
Isaiah 54	➤ The seed for a Covenant of Peace and Prosperity	$54
Isaiah 55: 5	➤ The seed for Abundant Life and Restoration	$55.05, $555
Isaiah 60: 17 – 18	➤ 60: 17 – Prosperity on a Nation / Peace With Politicians, Nation Leaders Church Leaders & Businesses ➤ 60:18 – Righteousness and Production Increase	$60.17 $60.18
Isaiah 10: 27	The seed for the anointing to destroy the yoke. This includes financial, mental or physical yokes – things that keep you in bondage. *Noteworthy* A day is coming when woes will end, the Five-fold offices will function again to deliver God's people; in the same way that God delivered the people under Moses, and with Joshua in Judges 7: 25	$10.27

Scripture	Explanation	Amount
Psalm 105: 15 – 20	➤ The seed for release for those that are suffering – those that were under the yoke. *Noteworthy* To those who suffer for character development it is time for your release and judgement on the enemies. The term *'release'* means *'set free, liberate, unfastened, allowed to move from a fixed position, made available, deliverance from the rights of another, spiritual or natural blessing loosed'* A season of judgement and divine justice is coming upon all the nations around Israel; and *Israel* refers to the people of God. A time is coming when God will increase, He will bring salvation to His people and punishment to the rebellious. He will restore His righteous order on earth. God's people will rise and cast down un-Godly spiritual forces.	$105.15, $105.20
Psalm 20: 2 – 4	➤ For Strength and help from the Sanctuary ➤ For God to remember your offerings	$20.02, $20.03, $20.04

Scripture	Explanation	Amount
Isaiah 11: 2	➢ For Godly wisdom, counsel, might, knowledge and understanding to be upon you ➢ That the Spirit of the Lord be upon you	**$11.02, $1,102**
Psalm 112	A Seed for God to release a Comprehensive Blessing ➢ That your descendants will be mighty on the earth and the generation of the upright be blessed ➢ For wealth and riches to be in your house ➢ That there will be light in darkness for you ➢ That God will be gracious and compassionate and righteous toward you ➢ That God will guide your affairs with discretion ➢ That you will never be shaken ➢ That you will be in everlasting remembrance ➢ That you will not be afraid of evil tidings and your heart will be steadfast, trusting in the Lord ➢ That you will see your desire upon your enemies ➢ That you will be able to give to the poor ➢ That your horn will be exalted with honor and the wicked will see it and grieve ➢ That the desire of the wicked shall perish	**$112**

Chapter 27

II CHRONICLES 1 AND I KINGS 3

These Scriptures are important for the New Millionaire to understand, because they speak of the wisdom given by God to those who seek after it and the wealth that is added when Godly wisdom is sought. It is in fact, the wisdom of God that gives you riches and wealth. This Scripture helps us to recognize:

➤ That a seed is what moves God to give you wisdom and wealth – II Chronicles 1: 6

➤ After sowing your seed don't be afraid to ask God for what you want from Him – II Chronicles 6: 7

➤ Solomon asked God for the mercy He extended to David – II Chronicles 1: 8

➤ Solomon understood that burnt offering was only to be offered in a place where the Lord God chose – II Chronicles 1: 6 (See also Deuteronomy 12: 13 – 14)

➤ Solomon asked for wisdom and knowledge to judge the people God placed him over – II Chronicles 1: 10 (See also I Kings 3: 9)

➤ God is the one who determines the measure of blessing you receive based on what is in your heart – II Chronicles 1: 12. Further to this, according to verse 11, you must know your place of blessing – your Gibeon – in the end time. Interestingly, it is in verse 12 that you see that God is the One Who blessed Solomon Himself.

➤ God is the One Who strengthens and exalts you in the Kingdom – II Chronicles 1: 1

➤ God gave Solomon a wise and understanding heart – I Kings 3: 12

➤ When your heart is right and you please God, He always gives you additional things that you didn't even ask for – II Chronicles 1: 11 and I Kings 3: 13

➤ God always lengthens your days based on your keeping His instructions – I Kings 3: 14

➤ God spoke and made the prophetic promise to Solomon in a dream, and He still does so today. God does not use anyone without a prophetic utterance being declared – I Kings 3: 5 – 15. Similarly, in Genesis 15: 1 – 6, God made the Promise to Abraham in a dream.

➤ God always makes a covenant and gives blessing and impartation in a dream – I Chronicles 1: 7 – 12. Similarly, in Genesis 27: 10: 22 Jacob's dreams emphasized God's initiating grace as He assures him that He is Lord of the past, present and future. Jacob became the third (3rd) generation to receive the promise of the Abrahamic Covenant.

From the days of old until this present era, God's Principles have brought many into great places and great wealth. He desires that you follow these principles and examples so that you too may experience the fullness of His blessings and walk in true wealth.

The Poor And Needy To Kingly Status

While Solomon was the son of a king, and ultimately became a king, it is important for us to know that God will also bless and use the poor and needy and promote them to kingly status.

In Psalm 113: 6, God humbled Himself to behold the things that are in the heavens and in the earth. Jesus gave His life, which was humility, to behold the things that are in heaven and earth that you may receive the blessing.

In Psalm 113: 7 – 8, the Lord reveals that He raises up the poor out of the dust and lifts the need out of the ash heap, that He may seat him with princes of His people.

God sees everyone, according to Genesis 16 – the poor, rejected, needy and forgotten and He is their God. Even the Egyptian slave and her son, God blessed and multiplied their descendants exceedingly. The Lord always hears our afflictions and sees us. He is *Beer Lahai Roi* – the God Who Sees Me.

> ➤ Joshua 2: 4 and 6: 17 speak of Rahab, the prostitute who became the great-great-grandmother of a king – King David.

> ➢ The book of Ruth speaks of the Moabitess, an insignificant foreigner from a tribe that was despised by the Israelites, who became the great grandmother of one of Israel's greatest kings – King David.

Therefore, the pauper you ignore today, may be the New Millionaire you give honor to tomorrow!

Chapter 28

TITHING

The term *'tithe'* means *'one tenth'* and is hence derived from the word *'ten'*. The number 'ten' from a Biblical standpoint signifies *'divine economy, God's divine law, His eternal injunction and status'*. This is the number representative of the injunction of divine government.

The Meaning Of Ten And Purpose Of Tithe

Ten (10) is the Creator's portion, demanded by Him for the blessing He has to give us.

The Tithe is your security, your insurance policy payment. It covers you from destruction, devastation, waste, sickness and it will also prevent the devourer – which is the devil – from attacking you, your company, your family or your nation.

The principle of Tithing began in Genesis with a military victory against the enemy – according to Genesis 14 and 15 concerning the Promise.

Those who Tithe automatically have a covenant with God.

You can't be a true worshipper if you don't Tithe. Worshipping is giving and it acknowledges that God is the One Who is totally in charge. He is the One Who provides and He is the One Who allows you to reap a harvest.

In the days of old, only the poor and the slaves who were captives did not bring the tithe; the poor because they did not have a job (Amos 6: 4 - 6). But God altered it and said ALL. It is not only the rich and prosperous that must tithe, but all must tithe.

The number *'ten'*, according to Daniel 5: 27 and Revelations 2: 10, also means *'rich, prove, weight, measure, accept or reject'*. Test to see if you will pass or fail.

A person who does not tithe has immediately failed the test; and failure will be rejected. If you can't pass a test by paying a tithe from \$100 or \$10, how can God promote you so that you can tithe from \$1000 or \$10,000.

A person who refuses to Tithe is not sold out to God, and He does not control that person's heart. The money you refuse to give is therefore your god.

Ten (10) is the number governments use. It is the number of judgement. God unleashed ten (10) plagues on Egypt because they were not honoring God with their resources. They were honoring other gods including Isis, Seth and Hator. So God was showing them that He is the God of multiplication and increase and that He caused the rain to fall and bring about prosperity.

The same thing can be found in I Kings 17 and 18. The Israelites were not acknowledging God, and honoring Him with their resources, so there was a recession on the nation. (See also Haggai 1 and 2)

God is always in charge of the nations' economies and also of your finance. No-one or no nation can say that they serve the true and living God and they don't tithe – as is found in Malachi 3: 10. If God gets your heart, He will not have a problem to release money to you. Recognize and understand that God's storehouse is on earth. That is where His ministers carry out His business affairs.

If God's business starts to make a loss, because you refuse to give, your company, business and you will make a loss until God gets your attention.

The moment God's leaders, especially His priests and apostles, are being neglected, and are unable to live on what comes through ministry; and once tithes are not enough to live on and they begin to wander in order to survive, or enter into idolatrous relationships in order to survive, then there will be judgement on the individual, city or nation.

There are many persons who are not even in a relationship with God, not having yielded their lives to Him, but they understand the principle of taking care of the Priests of the House of God. In Judges 17: 7 – 13, the Levite in this Scripture was seeking a place to reside temporarily. Micah knew the blessing he would receive to have a father and a priest to advise him, because he knew the importance of this kind of relationship. In verse 10, Micah agreed to pay the Levite to be his priest. He offered to pay him ten (10) shekels of silver year, a clothing allowance and other benefits to be his priest/father/apostle because he knew the blessing that would come.

Even the Pharaoh did it when he employed Joseph, in Genesis 45: 8, as a father/apostle/manager/advisor and a Prime Minister; and look at the blessing God gave to Pharaoh. Micah knew that if he had one of God's servants as a priest to Him – a father/apostle, great blessing would be upon him. (See also Judges 18: 4)

When you have a priest in your corner, he will pray for you, inquire of God for you. For example, he can pray concerning your business decisions, deals and all your transactions. He will pray blessings on you when you give him a Tithe from your blessing, as in Genesis 14 with Abraham, and he became priest. Adopt a man or woman of God and be a blessing to them that God will release blessings to you.

The Tithing Principle – I Corinthians 9

As you read I Corinthians 9, Paul here lists his rights as a minister. He outlined all the categories – soldiers, farmer, shepherd and so on – how they live from their profession. They must receive remuneration!

I Corinthians 9: 9, Paul speaks about the Laws of Moses; you shall not muzzle an ox while it treads out the grain. It also outlined in the Miscellaneous Laws found in Deuteronomy 25: 4 and Proverbs 12: 10 that any kind of muzzle will bring great suffering to a nation. God intended that His servants live from the Gospel. Once the leadership within a nation imposes laws that will come against His church, it is the spirit of the anti-Christ at work.

Understand that the purpose of these laws is to ensure that:

➢ The church does not benefit from the Tax Exempt Status

➢ The leaders don't have the necessary funds to preach the gospel, hence they cannot be a part of the full-time ministry

Hence, there will be no one to tend the flock; neither will there be any revelations to break down evil.

Nehemiah realized this – so did Ezra – so they brought back restoration to this area so that the blessing would return to the nation. See II Chronicles 31 regarding Hezekiah.

Deuteronomy 27 speaks about the Law of Tithing. You have undoubtedly seen many nations impose laws, but have never seen any country impose Tithing as a law. Yet, this is God's command and this command must be obeyed. There can be no blessing, particularly on a nation, unless this command is obeyed. With all the laws imposed in the nations, refusal to Tithe will result in the failure of the effectiveness of the other laws imposed; because the success of all the other laws within the nations depends on Malachi 3: 8 - 12.

➢ It speaks about robbing God – which is a crime

➢ It speaks about being cursed with a curse

➢ It speaks that the whole nation will also be cursed

➢ It speaks that you should bring in the Tithes to the storehouse, which is the church, so that there would be food in His House – "... *And prove me now in this...*" Malachi 3: 10

➢ It speaks of God opening the windows of heaven. That means heaven has more than one window through which God blesses His people. So much so that there will not be room enough to receive it.

God will rebuke the devourer for your sake so that he will not destroy the fruit of your ground. *"'...Nor shall the vine fail to bear fruit, for you in the field,' says the Lord of Hosts; 'And all nations will call you blessed you will be a delightful land' says the Lord of Hosts."* Malachi 3:11 - 12

As you read the Scriptures Daniel 8: 9 – 13 and Daniel 7: 25, recognize that those ten (10) leaders of nations will come together, they will impose laws against the church:

➢ Taxes

➢ Flex Week

➢ Zoning

➢ Prevention of certain licenses

They will be backed by religious spirits, judicial systems to carry their onslaught against the church. They will implement laws that Pastors will have to seek other employment, as the church will not be a source.

God wants his people to use the format of the book of Acts that there will be no lack – as in Acts 4: 32 – 37 and Acts 2: 40 – 47 so that His mandate can be accomplished.

Refusal To Tithe

Refusal to pay Tithes is rejecting God as king, but you will have to pay the earthly king's taxes, as in I Samuel 8: 11 – 17, because you became a slave to the systems of bondage and debt. God wants us to be free to serve Him, not to be in debt. That is why you have to add a fifth part to it if you withhold God's just due. You, the borrower, will serve the lender according to Leviticus 27: 31 and Proverbs 22: 7.

You must serve God only, not the lender. It is time to come out of bondage, out of debt. Recognize that that:

➢ The Tithe is holy to the Lord – Leviticus 27: 30 – 33 – as a result

➢ A non-tither is not holy or consecrated to God – Leviticus 27

Jesus paid with His Tithe – His life to redeem you from bondage, from sin. To *'redeem'* means *'to buy back, to recover by expenditure of effort or by stipulated payment, charge or obligation'*. It also means *'to convert token or bond into goods or cash, deliver from sin or damnation, save a person's life by ransom'*. Why do people want to go back to sin?

Tithing and Revival

Tithing brings revival to a nation and the Church, as is revealed in II Chronicles 31: 5 – 12; Nehemiah 10: 37 – 38 and Nehemiah 12: 43 – 47. Revival can come in the form of

➢ New business

➢ New investments

➢ Growth

➢ Improved economy

The seven (7) principles of tithing found in Malachi 3: 10 reveals to us that failure to tithe will lead to:

➢ Recession

➢ Poverty

➢ Chaos

➢   Bankruptcy

Let us look at Hezekiah, and II Chronicles 31: 2, and what he did to bring reformation and revival in the nation's economy.

He commanded the people who dwelled in Jerusalem or contributed support for the priest and Levites that they might devote themselves to the laws of the land. In Acts 2 and Acts 4 they laid the offerings at the apostles' feet that they could be given to the word and prayer.

Additionally, according to Malachi 2: 7, God states that

"... the lips of a priest should keep knowledge, and people should seek the law from his mouth; for he is the messenger of the Lord of hosts."

He is God's messenger to individuals, organizations and nations. (See also Galatians 4: 13 – 15 and Numbers 18: 8)

When God's ministers are going through financial problems, they can't seek God the way they should. Then the Church and the nations feel the effect because there is no fresh revelation from God! This is what is happening now!

In II Chronicles 31: 5 – 7, look at what happens in the third month as they obeyed the instructions. In verse 8, the king blessed the Lord and His people Israel; and in verse 9, the king questioned the priest concerning the heaps. The heaps were the tithes. In verse 10, he receives the answer.

"And Azariah the chief priest from the house of Zadok answered him and said, 'Since the people began to bring the offerings into the house of the Lord, we have had enough to eat and have plenty left, for the Lord has blessed His people and what is left is this great abundance.'"

You are reminded of the same thing in Malachi 3: 10 and Exodus 36: 5.

Further in II Chronicles 31: 11, Hezekiah commanded that rooms be prepared in the House of the Lord that the nations would be blessed. In their faithfulness, they sanctified themselves unto holiness and in verse 21, the result was that the king and the nation prospered.

Lead By Example

God's people must first do business with a *'Tither'* (one who pays Tithes) so that the money will stay in the Kingdom. God's people must lead by example, your tithes and offerings first so that those who are unsaved will follow the good example.

In Nehemiah 13, the number *'10'* speaks of the *'Restoration of Levitical support'*. In this Scripture, you see that the priests and singers/worshippers had to go back to their secular jobs, because there was no support for them.

Many ministers and musicians are going back to their secular jobs and are giving up because there is no support and sustenance. Nehemiah 10: 37 reveals that you need to give the firstfruits of our money and the tithe – even the farming community should bring so that there will be blessing. What the priests receive, they should tithe from it, according to Nehemiah 10: 38 and I Chronicles 9: 26. Neglect of the House of God must stop! (See Nehemiah 10: 39)

If the leader is swimming in financial problems, then you at the bottom of the hierarchy will also swim in it!

The New Testament On Tithing

I Corinthians 9: 6 – 7 remind you of the yield you receive when you sow/give.

GIVE	MEANING	RECEIVE
Sparingly	Restrain in giving	Limited Blessings
Bountifully	Generous in giving	Abundant & Generous blessings
Cheerfully	Give in good spirit, Happy Bright, pleasant; willingly and not reluctantly	Abundant Blessings with great joy

Motives For Giving

A person's motive for giving is key! Your gifts don't make God wealthier, but it makes you richer – spiritually and naturally.

Motives speak of the reason a person does what he/she does. It asks the question, *'Why are you giving to God?'* If you love God or His servants, you won't have a problem giving, because God is Love! He personifies and exemplifies love!

I Corinthians 16: 2 and Hebrews 7 reveal that Jesus is your High Priest to Whom you tithe; and for a better covenant.

The Tithe Is Holy

Leviticus 27: 30 and Genesis 28: 22 speak of the holiness of the tithe. Only holy hands must touch the holy things. If a person is not paying tithes, he is not holy, whether:

➤ Treasurer

➤ Greeter

➤ Usher

➤ Pastor

He/She should not touch the tithes, because then, the tithes would no longer be holy.

While grace has been extended to all mankind, grace must not be taken for granted. Haggai 2: 11 – 14 explains that the amalgamation of clean and unclean cannot and does not work. Further to this, in I Chronicles 13: 6 – 11 and II Samuel 6: 6 - 11, you see what happens to those who touch the things that have been consecrated to the Lord.

God's people should always give preference to those who tithe when doing business. You would not want to be in partnership with one who says he/she loves God but refuses to tithe. This would be un-Scriptural.

Also, in Leviticus 27: 32 – 33, you see that, farmers and those in agriculture and livestock must tithe. Failure to do so will result in world famine, disasters, food shortage and none will be exempt.

What nations should do is reduce taxes and increase tithes and you would see financial revival and economic growth in a nation, just as is seen in II Chronicles 31. Additionally, those countries that are in debt, once they practice this principle of tithing and sowing seed (giving offerings and donations), God would give debt write-offs and revive the nation's economy. If they withhold the tithes, then they will not receive the seven (7) benefits that God promised.

Chapter 29

FIRST FRUITS

Proverbs 3: 9 – 10

You must honor the Lord with the first fruit of your increase! This includes:

➤ Salary

➤ The first job you did/do, it belongs to God

➤ The first child you receive from the Lord must be dedicated to the Lord in a special way

Exodus 22: 29 tells us:

"You shall not delay to offer the first of your ripe produce and your juices. The firstborn of your sons you shall give to Me."

Exodus 23: 15 – 19 also say:

"You shall keep the Feast of Unleavened Bread (you shall eat unleavened bread seven days, as I commanded you, at the time appointed in the month of Abib, for in it you came out of Egypt; none shall appear before Me empty); and the Feast of Harvest, the firstfruits of your labors which you have sown in the field; and the Feast of Ingathering at the end of the year, when you have gathered in the fruit of your labors from the field. Three times in the year all your males shall appear before the Lord God. You shall not offer the blood of My sacrifice with leavened bread; nor shall the fat of My sacrifice remain

until morning. The first of the firstfruits of your land you shall bring into the house of the Lord"

There are three (3) times each year that the three (3) feasts must be celebrated and each person shall sow accordingly:

- ➢ April

- ➢ May – June

- ➢ September – June

According to Exodus 34: 22 – 24, when you observe what the Lord will do, when you obey the Feasts God will:

- ➢ Cast out nations before you

- ➢ Enlarge your borders

- ➢ Disallow jealousy coming against you

According to verse 26 He will also give you:

- ➢ New Business Ideas

- ➢ New Territory

- ➢ New Staff

- ➢ Expansion in every area

> Victory over your competitors who are against you

God will as in Exodus 33: 2 send angels to drive out your enemies when you obey Him with your giving. There are certain enemies who cannot be removed, unless you obey God with your giving He will drive them out. Once a person disobeys God in His instructions regarding giving, it is a sin and sin will bring punishment.

There are certain dimensions of blessings you cannot receive unless you give to the Lord. Exodus 34: 19 -20 tell you:

"All that open the womb are Mine, and every male firstborn among your livestock whether ox or sheep. But the firstborn of a donkey you shall redeem with a lamb. And if you will not redeem him, then you shall break his neck. All the firstborn of your sons shall you redeem. And none shall appear before Me empty-handed."

The first born sons belonged to God in a special way because He spared them in Egypt, they were to be as the first fruit offering to God.

Law Of The Firstborn

Exodus 34: 11 – 16 is the Law Of The First Born.

"Observe what I command you this day. Behold, I am driving out from before you the Amorite and the Canaanite and the Hittite and the Perizzite and the Hivite and the Jebusite. Take heed to yourself, lest you make a covenant with the inhabitants

of the land where you are going, lest it be a snare in your midst. But you shall destroy their altars, break their sacred pillars, and cut down their wooden images (for you shall worship no other god, for the Lord, whose name is Jealous, is a jealous God), lest you make a covenant with the inhabitants of the land, and they play the harlot with their gods and make sacrifice to their gods, and one of them invites you and you eat of his sacrifice, and you take of his daughters for your sons, and his daughters for your sons play the harlot with their gods."

This instruction is for all it is not just for individuals, nations and administration. If they were following the instructions of God, especially in the parliament of each nation, each country would be blessed.

Exodus 12: 36 says:

"And the Lord had given the people favor in the sight of the Egyptians, so that they granted them what they requested. Thus they plundered the Egyptians."

Exodus 13: 1 – 2 show you how serious God is regarding *'Firsts'* – man, beast, jobs and so on.

"Then the Lord spoke to Moses, saying, 'Consecrate to Me all the firstborn, whatever opens the womb among the children of Israel, both of man and beast; it is Mine.'"

All must be consecrated to the Lord! Once this takes place, blessing will follow.

The firstborn of Egypt had not been dedicated to the true and living God, so God struck them. God gave the Israelites favor with the prized possessions of the Egyptians.

Exodus 11: 3 tells us:

"And the Lord gave the people favor in the sight of the Egyptians. Moreover the man Moses was very great in the land of Egypt, in the sight of the people."

That means, just as God gave Moses favor with the Egyptians, He will do the same for us. Additionally, for favor with Egypt, the Exodus 12: 36 Seed should be sown. This seed is to get their favor and wealth.

According to Ezekiel 44: 30, the best of the firstfruits of any kind shall be given to the priests to cause a blessing to rest on your house.

"The best of all firstfruits of any kind, and every sacrifice of any kind from all your sacrifices, shall be the priest's; also you shall give to the priest the first of your ground meal, to cause a blessing to rest on your house."

The following Scriptures also give a better understanding of how God looks at the firstborn:

> ➤ Numbers 3: 13 (All firstborn are for God)

> ➤ Leviticus 27: 26 (No debates or dictates)

> ➤ Numbers 8: 16 – 17

Luke 2: 22 – 23 state:

"Now when the days of her purification according to the law of Moses were completed, they brought Him to Jerusalem to present Him to the Lord (as it is written in the law of the Lord,

'Every male who opens the womb shall be called holy to the Lord'),"

Additionally, Leviticus 27: 30 – 31 say:

"*And all the tithe of the land, whether of the seed of the land or of the fruit of the tree, is the Lord's. It is holy of the Lord. If a man wants at all to redeem any of his tithes, he shall add one-fifth to it.*"

Leviticus 23: 9 – 12 say:

"*And the Lord spoke to Moses, saying, 'Speak to the children of Israel, and say to them: 'When you come into the land which I give to you, and reap its harvest, then you shall bring a sheaf of the firstfruits of your harvest to the priest. He shall wave the sheaf before the Lord, to be accepted on your behalf; on the day after the Sabbath the priest shall wave it. And you shall offer on that day, when you wave the sheaf, a male lamb of the first year, without blemish, as a burnt offering to the Lord.*"

The Law Concerning Firstborn Animals

Deuteronomy 15: 19 – 23 speak of the Law concerning firstborn animals. It says:

"*All the firstborn males that come from your herd and your flock you shall sanctify to the Lord your God; you shall do no work with the firstborn of your herd, nor shear the firstborn of your flock. You and your household shall eat it before the Lord your God year by year in the place which the Lord chooses. But if there is a defect in it, if it is lame or blind or has any serious defect, you shall not sacrifice it to the Lord your God.*

You may eat it within your gates; the unclean and the clean person alike may eat it, as if it were a gazelle or a deer. Only you shall not eat its blood; you shall pour it on the ground like water."

There are several additional laws found in the word of God.

> ➤ The Law of Tithe   Deuteronomy 26

> ➤ The Law of Debt   Deuteronomy 15: 1 – 11

> ➤ The Law of Feasts   Deuteronomy 16: 1 – 17

All Firstfruits To The House - Nehemiah 10

Once you enter into a covenant with God, there are certain things to which you must adhere.

> ➤ No mixed marriages – that means, partners **must not be unequally yoked**

> ➤ Keep God's day of worship

> ➤ Give proper care of God's temple (Haggai 2)

> ➤ Be set apart. People who serve God must be set apart. Priests, Levites, must obey His laws and do His will

> ➤ Instructions regarding marriage for their sons and daughters.

> ➤ Hallow the Sabbath. They should not buy or sell, for example, carry out business on God's holy days or on the Sabbath

> ➤ Give debt write-offs every seven (7) years

Also they would give one-third of a shekel, for the service of our God. They would obey all the feasts and offerings and they would give to the house of God for God's work to be done.

For any nation or individual to be blessed, God has to speak to their hearts regarding giving. Once God gets their heart to obey then serious blessings will come. Obedience is the key to blessing. His house must be taken care of.

God does not want His ministers - those who minister in His house – to be working in other places as well. He wants them to seek Him, for divine revelation to deal with the needs of God's servants, so that the blessings will rest on their house, according to Galatians 6: 6 – 7

Paul applies the general principles of sowing and reaping to the support of Christian Teachers for

Verses 8 – 10 reveal that what you sow you reap. He also instructions us to do good, especially to those who are of the household of faith. Once you find good soil, sow that the man or woman of God can intercede for you, for the blessing of God to be on your household.

If all businesses and government officials were obeying the word and applying spiritual Biblical instruction, then there would have already been healing and restoration to many situations. The fact is there is a resistance to applying Godly principles. Why? They know it will work, so the enemy doesn't want God to take the glory. The time is coming when all nations, will see the whole earth filled with the glory of God (Habakkuk 2: 14) and the knowledge of God.

In the same way that taxes are imposed and it is a law to pay certain taxes, there needs to be a law implemented as in Nehemiah 10: 32 to regulate a steady income differently, for the sanctuary on a yearly basis.

To be blessed they must also obey the First Fruit Principle – all belongs to God. Tithes, Money, Farming, New wine/oil to the priests, who would in turn give back to the House ten percent (10%)

In no way must the House of God be neglected, Deuteronomy 12: 6 & 11, also II Chronicles 31 regarding the reforms of Hezekiah. He knew that by reforming a nation there must be a gathering of all the Tithes (verses 11 – 12). Because he sought God with all his heart, he prospered; he did what was right and good and true.

The devil knows that once he can get the priests to lose focus of the things of God because of a lack of support, they cannot fully devote themselves to the things of God and as a result, the nation will suffer.

Hezekiah knew that he had to bring restoration to this area for the economy to return; he got the priests to resume their duties; he got the people to give their tithes and offerings. That was why his administration was prosperous.

Hezekiah led in order to bring reformation, and exemplified by giving out of his own possessions. David did the same thing when he was building the temple in the book of Chronicles for reformation within the nation. Leaders need to look on the life of Hezekiah!

II Chronicles 31: 7 the third month which is March to July is the seasons for carrying out God's mandate to be blessed.

Once the Lord's true servants have enough to eat because of their obedience - II Chronicles 31: 10 says:

"Then there will be great abundance, as the Lord will bless His people."

The Lord truly wants to bless His people, but they do not want to walk in obedience, and only those who do, will benefit.

Facts About First Fruits

According to Nehemiah 10: 32 – 37 and Ezekiel 44: 30:

> ➢ Always have a spiritual advisor – a deep, true holy man or woman of God. They will give you advice, direction on personal and business

> matters, and will pray that your business transactions will come forth. For example, the Scriptures show that Daniel, Joseph, Nehemiah and Ezra all walked in the Governmental Anointing!

> Blessing a man or woman of God that he/she can devote himself or herself to the work of God will bring great blessing to you, and your administration; Hezekiah realized that in II Chronicles 31 he gave from His personal possession and he was blessed!

> Your First Fruit means that once you get an increase of salary – it must go to your priest/spiritual advisors. First fruits can come from New Contracts, New businesses, the first sales. Even if you are not attending a church, you must pay your Tithes according to Malachi 3: 10 to where the Lord place, in Your Spirit (Deuteronomy 12) to get your blessing!

How To Pray For Prosperity

Psalm 133 and Psalm 35 tell us that God is a God of order. Therefore, He is going to cause the church to prosper beginning from the local church. The local church must ensure that their leaders prosper in every area of their lives. So:

- ➢ Pray for the prosperity of your leaders

- ➢ Pray for daily favor upon them including favor in the area of business

- ➢ Pray that they will be billionaires and there will be no lack among them

- ➢ Pray that people will give to them on a daily basis by sowing seed to them – including money, vehicles, houses, land and clothes and other things for their families

- ➢ Pray that you who are praying will be the first to sow

Remember:

- ➢ When your leader is blessed it will flow down to the entire congregation

- ➢ It is difficult to have unity in poverty

- ➢ God takes pleasure in the prosperity of His people (Psalm 35: 27)

- ➢ Adversity brings great stress and ill-health on God's people. The longer you stay in poverty, the richer the medical and pharmaceutical industries become at your expense.

Therefore:

> ➤ Pray that the stronghold over your area or church
> will come down and that the stronghold that
> opposes the message of prosperity will also come
> down; that people will give freely to God's
> servants, to His house and into His Kingdom

> ➤ Pray that the people will not put God's House on
> hold while they build their own houses, as in
> Haggai 1: 7. They need to build God's house that
> God will not withhold the blessings.

When you fail to build God's House financially, it will
bring famine – economic problems on the nation. There
will be recession and oppression. This, according to
Haggai 1: 11, is what is happening now and God's work
has been neglected in the nations. Everyone is too busy
doing his/her own thing. People are building, but not
God's House! When there is famine in a nation, it comes
right down to the state of faithfulness in a church and in
the nations, according to Haggai 1: 9, which says:

*"'You looked for much, but indeed it came to little; and when
you brought it home, I blew it away. Why?' says the Lord of
hosts; because of My house that is in ruins, while every one of
you runs to his own house.'"*

God wants His leaders to work full time, that He can use
them to transform nations, according to II Chronicles 31:
4.

Chapter 30

MINISTERIAL COMPENSATION

The compensation of Ministerial personnel has been an issue for many years and even more so now. But the Bible reveals the principle as a guideline. The general principle is found in Luke 10.

Any employment that deals with the following must attract compensation at the highest level:-

➤ The saving of souls for God

➤ Directing and leading others toward everlasting life through the daily application of Biblical Principle

➤ Bringing out the individual's purpose to fulfillment in line with God's perfect plan

➤ Ministering to the lives of individuals

➤ Ministering peace on earth through Christ

➤ Ministering to the Spiritual and natural needs of the individual

➤ Presenting the Gospel as the most important product on earth and is a salesman for the Kingdom of God

➢ Declaring Life as a gift from God and that having everlasting life is the most important thing above life

OR

Anyone who:

➢ Is a salesman for Christ undergoing the most dangerous threats for the sake of their product – the Gospel.

➢ Builds the Kingdom of God to impact nations for Kingdom rule

➢ Is a genuine agent of God communicating to the earthly realm what the Spirit of the Lord is saying.

must receive remuneration at the highest level.

Jesus clearly outlines in Matthew 10: 40 – 42 the various rewards and blessings each person will would receive as he/she blesses a servant of God. The reason certain blessings cannot be realized on earth is as a result of the lack of giving to Godly authority. Look at what I Kings 17: 8 – 24, II Kings 4: 8 – 37 and Genesis 14: 18 – 24 have to say concerning this matter.

Giving to the Kingdom can change your career or destiny, according to Luke 5: 1 – 11. In fact, one harlot's entire life was changed, in Joshua 6: 17 – 19, and she became great. Rahab, by simply extending kindness to God's agent, saved her household and became the great grand-mother of King David, and engrafted in the lineage of Jesus.

A person who is not excited to give or about giving to God does not understand what love is. Jesus is Love and He showed us love by giving His life, yielding to the cross for us, as is shown in John 3: 16.

The Kingdom of Heaven is about sowing – giving – as is revealed in Galatians 6: 7 and Job 4: 8. Therefore, nothing sown yields a harvest of nothing!

When you ask God for a harvest, He asks you for a seed. In Genesis 15: 1 – 10, Abraham was childless and he sought God for a child to continue his lineage and to whom he would pass on the inheritance. Verse 9 reveals to us that every promise God makes to you, you must put a seed in the *'ground'*, because He gives nothing without something with which to defend your harvest.

Genesis 1: 12 says that every seed contains an instruction. Your seed is always your way out of trouble. Look also at II Samuel 24: 25. Further to this, as you read, Mark 10: 29 – 30, you will realize that an uncommon seed carries with it a potentially major harvest.

Now, for the windows of heaven to open, you must first do as Malachi 3: 10 instructs and bring in your Tithes to the storehouse – your local church!

Remember that your seed is any tool God has given you to create your future. As such, there are different types of seed including:

- ➢ Extending Love
- ➢ Intercession
- ➢ Money

➢   Spending Time
➢   Showing Mercy
➢   Extending Favor

There is always something to sow; even your obedience in following instructions from God through man, as is found in I Kings 17, II Kings 4: 1 – 7. By obeying the instructions of the man of God, the women received debt write-offs and miracles in the time of famine.

Your seed can create a miracle to feed many and bring a great harvest, according to John 6: 1 – 14. Five (5) Barley loaves and two (2) small fish fed a great multitude.

God wants lawyers, doctors, scientists, teachers and other professionals to sow their time – no charge – as a seed. In Genesis 40: 5 – 23, Joseph gave free consultation by interpreting dreams free of charge! That was his seed, and look at the harvest he received as a result.

Luke 13: 18 – 19 and Matthew 13: 31 – 32 reveals that the Kingdom of God is like a mustard seed. This is one of the smallest seeds of the plant world; and when put in your garden has the potential to grow and become as large as a tree. A mustard seed is the least of all seeds, but when it grows, it is greater than the other herbs.

Interestingly your seed will find you when you least expect it. Your harvest will spring forth. As a result of the seed he sowed to the butler and the baker in Genesis 41: 14, Joseph was brought before the Pharaoh – the one with absolute earthly authority to release him. Ultimately, his seed brought him freedom and promotion.

A Moabitess widow by the name of Ruth, a foreigner had been married to one of the sons of a Hebrew woman. After being given the blessing and release by her mother-in-law Naomi, chose by faith to stay with her vowing never to leave her. She sowed a seed by serving Naomi and ended up with a massive harvest by the name of Boaz! The seed continued to bring her great harvest not only in the form of great wealth and high social standing in the community, but caused her to be the grandmother of a great king – David and as such, a part of the lineage of Jesus!

By sowing the seed of kindness, you never know who will take note of the kindness you have done and what kind of favor it will bring you in the future. That is evident in Ruth 2: 10 -11. Because of the seed she sowed in the kingdom through the kindness she showed, it brought her to reap in Boaz's field, not as an ordinary person but as a future landowner and royalty – Ruth 2: 13 – 17.
It is interesting to note that the gleaning law forbade foreigners to reap the corners of the fields or gather the gleaning of the harvest, according to Leviticus 19: 9 and 22 – 23. It was in fact to be left for the poor and strangers. But Ruth went from *gleaning* to *reaping*! In Ruth 2: 14, Boaz acknowledged her at mealtime by inviting her to sit with the reapers; a privilege the average gleaner enjoyed. She received favor, according to Ruth 2: 15 - 16

Ruth 2: 15 -17 speak of Boaz's directive to the young men, to allow Ruth to garner far more than she could have otherwise.

God is the One Who opens doors and you never know to which field He may lead you from which you may glean and ultimately reap. (Ruth 2: 20)

Ruth's loyalty to Naomi and to God moved her to leave her own homeland of Moab for Judah. Though a foreigner, she became an ancestress of David, and of the Christ. (Luke 3: 31 – 32)

God always raises up outsiders and those considered to be the least, who are faithful to Him and support His people. Look at:

➢ Ruth
➢ Jabez
➢ Rahab
➢ Gideon
➢ Joseph
➢ David

A person's status, race, color, academic qualifications are irrelevant to God when He chooses who to lift up or promote. He looks at the level of their faithfulness and their obedience, particularly to the Seed Principle. God brought a Moabite into the circle of His own people and eventually into the royal line.

Hardship, indebtedness and famine sometimes lead you into royalty and greatness, as was seen with Ruth and Joseph.

Mentors And The Seed

God will always put people as mentors in your life to instruct you on how to prepare to receive greater favor and these mentors will seek security for you. This is what happened with Naomi and Ruth. Naomi became Ruth's mentor in Ruth 3: 1.

Your mentors will instruct you concerning the protocol requirements. For example:

> ➢ Potiphar was Joseph's mentor for a season, according to Genesis 39: 1 – 6 and he learnt how to function at that level. In Genesis 41: 14 he further learnt that he needed to shave his beard and change his clothing when going before the king, which were not done in his original culture.

> ➢ Ruth was instructed by her mentor to wash her hair and anoint herself – that is – put on the best garment, according to Ruth 3: 3. She further instructed Ruth not to make herself known until he had finished eating and drinking, in Ruth 3: 4. Naomi told her that after eating and drinking he will feel merry, happy and cheerful. This was protocol and wisdom, and her obedience to these instructions caused her to get great favor.

> ➢ Joab knew the protocol of King David and how to approach him, according to II Samuel 14: 2 – 3.

Always be submissive and obedient to the instructions of your mentors so that you will walk in favor, as was seen in Ruth 3: 5 - 6.

As a result, in Ruth 3: 11, Boaz realized that Ruth had the character of a virtuous woman.

How To Pray To Move Ahead In Ministry (Especially For God's Leaders)

Pray and ask God to:

> ➢ Give you people who will respect the anointing on your life

> ➢ Send you people who will be a blessing to you, not a curse.

> ➢ Send builders to you, not those who will tear down

> ➢ Send those with a servant's heart (*II Kings 2 – Elijah & Elisha*)

> ➢ Send laborers to your ministry

> ➢ Send people who will celebrate and promote your ministry (*II Kings 5 – The Young Slave Girl*)

> ➢ Send people who will assist your ministry (*Just as Jesus …. And Paul – Luke 8: 1 – 3.*

> ➢ Send many women to come into the ministry. (*Women are more willing to minister to the needs of God's servants – proven in I Kings 17 – Elijah & the Widow; Luke 10: 38 – 42 – Mary & Martha.*)

Luke 10: 33

God always sends help from despised sources. There was distinct racial strain between Jesus and the Samaritans, according to John 4: 9. The source of assistance was not a kinsman or fellow citizen of Israel, but a despised Samaritan!

In John 4, the Samaritan woman was the biggest celebration of Jesus' ministry as is seen in verse 29 – '...*Come see a man!*"

The transformed woman became a great evangelist, influencing her entire community and many Samaritans responded to Jesus' ministry. While the Jews rejected Him (vs 29-30 and 39-41), the Samaritans believed in Him because of the word of the woman who testified in verse 39 and in verses 40 – 42, they took Jesus' ministry to the next level.

A prostitute – in her line of business she knew all the affluent and influential persons based on her clientele and would bring them to Jesus' ministry and they would be a support to Jesus' ministry.

An un-named Samaritan woman received life-changing revelation that eludes many scholars. (I Corinthians 1: 26 – 29)

> ➢ She received Jesus as a Prophet

> ➢ She received Christ

> ➢ She discerned, but Christians would tear down!

One of the great tragedies of prejudice is that it may separate one from a potential source of assistance! The compassion of the Samaritan woman overshadowed her prejudice, because, under normal circumstances she probably would not have even spoken to Him! Christ came to break down such division. (James 2: 1 – 9)

In Matthew 27: 32, wise men of all ages would be honored if allowed, to perform the task that was conferred upon Simon of Cyrene - a black man from North Western Africa. The black hands were extended to help the Savior bear His cross. It was not the Jews, nor His own disciples.

The Ethiopian Eunuch in Acts 8: 26 was the first Gentile convert named in the book of Acts. He returned to Ethiopia to found the Abyssinian Christian Church – Ephesians 2: 1 – 10

Also, in I Kings 17, it was a widow to whom God sent the man of God. He did not send him to a person of higher status. God always uses the single persons to bless His people. It is for you to discern where He is opening the door!

In Mark 15: 40 – 41 you will see that most of Jesus' *'partners'*/ support came from women; so Jesus had Covenant Partners also, who traveled with Him.

Mary Magdalene was a steadfast disciple of Jesus and is best seen as a case study of how no dimension of Satanic bondage can prohibit individuals being restored to fruitful service for Christ. She helped and assisted Jesus' ministry.

Anna, a prophetess, an old widow of about eighty-four
(84) years, did not depart from the temple, but served
God with fasting and prayers night and day! The name
'Anna' means *'favor, grace'* or in Hebrew *'to bend or stoop
in kindness, find favor, show favor'*. She was obedient and
pure!
As you read Luke 4: 16 – 28, you will realize that those to
whom you are looking to respect the anointing are
oftentimes not those who will do so. In addition, you
must understand that your countrymen will not respect
or readily embrace your anointing. Neither will your
own family sometimes. Your own will always be
skeptics and will want to judge you by earthly
qualifications. They will not celebrate the anointing;
hence no great miracles will take place. Jesus speaks in
Luke 4: 24:

*"Then He said, 'Assuredly, I say to you, no prophet is accepted
in his own country.'"*

He also speaks that there were many widows in Israel on
the day of Elijah, during famine, but none of them, Elijah
was sent to except to Zarephath in the region of Sidon, to
a woman who was a widow. Why did He not send to
those others? Because He knew their hearts! He knew
they would not respect the anointing and support the
man of God's ministry. God used an outsider!

➢ Jesus was rejected by His own

➢ Joseph was rejected by his own

➢ Elijah was rejected by his own

➢ John was rejected by his own

➢ Jeremiah was rejected by his own

➢ Elisha was rejected by his own

In Luke 4: 25 - 27, the introduction of Elijah and Elisha in these verses not only explains why Jesus the Prophet, was rejected but also emphasizes the transfer of the kingdom, from rebellious Israel to the Gentiles! The two regions Zarephath, (Sidon -I Kings 17: 9) and Syria (II Kings 5: 1 – 14), are notably Gentile! They were not Israelites, God blessed them in Gentile territory. Many lepers (II Kings 5: 1 – 4) were in Israel in the time of Elisha and none of them were cleansed except Naaman the Syrian.

A prophet or a businessman will never be honored in his country. Each time God wants to bless you, whether with spiritual or natural investment, or people to support you, He sends you to a different place to a people who are not your own kind that they will appreciate and support you!

In Matthew 13: 53 – 58 Jesus clearly outlines the word 'HONOR'! It is difficult to get honor in your own country – whether it be from your relatives or your own church!

Unbelief will hinder mighty works, especially from your own, your vision is not among whom you think. God has a people who will honor and support you to be that great or new millionaire. (John 4: 43 -45)

Chapter 31

THINGS THAT CAN AFFECT A NATION FINANCIALLY

As you seek to understand the secrets to being a New Millionaire, you need to understand what affects the finances of our nation because it affects us.

1. Worshipping other gods and not seeking the true and living God. I Kings 18:21

2. Curses from past Administration – the evil/wrong things that they did – can affect the present and future Administration; according to II Samuel 21

3. A nation that no longer puts its trust in God in order to be successful in its economy or in wars is inviting plagues and famine upon the nation. When you begin to put your trust in man's carnal wisdom, instead of God's wisdom and direction, it causes serious problems.

4. If a country is not paying Tithes and offerings as a nation and on an individual level, according to Malachi 3: 8-12, this will bring a curse upon the nation and upon the people. Understand that refusal to Tithe will cause the windows of heaven to close and will block the blessing of God.

5. II Chronicles 31 breaks down images and sacred pillars. Bring in the offering and the nations will be blessed.

6. When the nation gives, the Lord blesses. If a nation is going through financial famine, the first thing to do is to call an amnesty as in II Chronicles 31. The leaders of the nation must lead by example II Chronicles 31: 2 – 3.

7. Malachi 2: 7 reveals to us that once financial problems affect God's leaders so much so that they cannot devote themselves fully to God and the work of God, it will affect the nation. (Read also Numbers 18: 8 – 9; Deuteronomy 17: 8 – 11) They will be judged as soon as the amnesty begins anywhere from March – July. In addition, the nation's Tithes and offerings must be collected. Verse 7 tells us to look on the blessing for obedience.

8. Exodus 36: 5 – 6 show that the people brought in so much offering that Moses had to command them to cease bringing the offerings.

9. Sins of God's priests can cause financial problems to a nation, as is found in Malachi 3: 2 – 3. God will purify them that they will offer to the Lord an offering in righteousness.

10. Malachi 3: 4 – 5 outline sins which can affect the finance of a nations:

    ✓ Offering that is polluted

    ✓ Sorcerers

    ✓ Adulterers

    ✓ Perjurers

Those who:

- ✓ Exploit wage earners, widows and the fatherless
- ✓ Turn away an alien
- ✓ Lack the fear of God

11. Malachi 1: 11 tells you that God wants pure, pleasing offerings

12. Malachi 1: 12 – 14 also outline the fact that God wants the best. Nothing profane or blemished not what is left. In those days they used to bring the stolen, lame and the sick to God as an offering.

13. Malachi 1: 7 – 8 state that they would offer defiled food on His altar. They offered the lame, sick and blind to God; and with tears, weeping and crying. In this Scripture, He says that He does not regard such offerings nor does He receive it with goodwill. Had you offered such poor offerings to your Governor would he be pleased with you? Would he accept you favorably?

Many want blessings, but they don't fear Him - they offer what they must offer to God to their governor. (They offer the silver, torn money. Not everyone's offering is accepted by God. Evil curses offerings)

The pollution of the nations, is outlined in Malachi 1: 6, where it tells us that the priests have lost all respect for God's name and in their greed, offer only diseased and

infected offering on the altar. They have more respect for the politicians than for the living God! God is withholding His blessings from such persons because of that and because of their disobedience to His covenant.
Malachi 2: 10 – 1 6 speak of men divorcing the wives of their youth in order to marry foreign women – and divorcing those wives for the wrong reasons. This will bring curses and cause God to withhold His blessing. God hates divorce. It covers one's garment with violence.

Malachi directs his message of judgement to a people plagued with corrupt priests wicked practices and a false sense of security in their privileged relationship with God – hypocrisy, infidelity, mixed marriages, divorce, false worship and arrogance. The nations, because they are so sinful, have neglected God's word concerning Tithing and giving of offerings. Look at Nehemiah 13: 10 – 14.

Realize that *'Nehemiahs'* bring restoration of Levitical support. They bring back the priests and the musicians who had gone back to secular work. This is evident in Nehemiah 10: 37 and Numbers 35: 2.

If the House of God is forsaken, this will bring a curse on the nations. He instructed all the people to bring the Tithes to the storehouse. Nehemiah 10: 38

Once the enemy, through financial problems, can get the leaders to get back to their secular positions/jobs, then he will dominate and control the nations through finance and neglect of God's House. This is what the enemy wants to do for evil to take over.

God wants to place His leaders back into full time service in ministry, wherein they will be paid to carry out God's work. Nehemiah 10: 38 and Nehemiah 12: 44.

Nehemiah appointed treasurers (Nehemiah 13: 13; I Corinthians 4: 2) to distribute to the faithful brethren.

As is found in Haggai 1: 4, neglecting God's house will cause great suffering on the land and its people!

Restoration of God's Day of Worship

Whether Saturday or Sunday, you must not profane God's day of worship. For example, flexi-week working denies God's people the opportunity to worship and will cause great financial problem. Look at Nehemiah 13: 20. Merchants and sellers are carrying out business transactions and ignoring God's days of worship; and it will backfire on a nation. Further to this, according to Nehemiah 13: 16, selling all kinds of things on God's days of worship will affect the economy in every way.

Restoration of Marriage

God's leaders are getting married to pagan wives, unsaved women, Nehemiah 13: 23 – 29. Take note of Nehemiah 13:26, which specifically speaks of this sin and its effect on the nations.

It therefore discourages people from continuing such practices, and instead encourages us to follow the Biblical Principles concerning Marriage in order to experience the blessings on the nation.

Chapter 32

HOW TO DISCERN WHEN JUDGEMENT IS ON A COMPANY, NATION OR CHURCH

Joel 1

The Book of Joel gives reference to locusts, and these creatures are symbolic of destruction; more specifically, mass destruction as a judgement from God!

Examples of 'locusts' in our midst include:

➤ Animals Dying Randomly

➤ Fires Burning Uncontrollably

➤ Flooding

➤ Drought

➤ Widespread Food Shortage

➤ Uncontrollable Crime & Violence

➤ Increase in Accidents

➤ Theft

➤ The Land being totally stripped

➢ Natural Disasters

➢ Killing of Children

➢ Price Increases

➢ Vegetation (trees, plant life) drying up

➢ Loss of husbands

➢ Lack of Growth

➢ High Level National Debt

➢ Bankruptcy

God always addresses His elders/prophets when things like these happen, and tells them to repent, take charge and to instruct nations in righteousness. Joel 1: 9 speaks of hardship on the church; lack of offering was a sign that God is judging churches and nations.

Grain, wine and oil were staples of the people's diet. Drought is a judgement from God. Additionally, verses 10 - 12 tells you what is considered the judgement of God. Joel 1: 13 - 14 explain that Ministers of Government must call a Fast in the nation and lie all night in sackcloth for the nation. Joel 1:17 - 18 give you further examples of judgement from God.

- ➤ Shortage of Food/Famine

- ➤ Destruction of crops, no first fruits or thank offering are available for use in expressing joy and gladness to the Lord.

- ➤ Mergers and business closures to reduce costs

- ➤ Widespread redundancies

- ➤ Low profit margins

When all this judgement is taking place, then God calls the nation to repentance, according to Joel 2: 12. He instructs the people to come before him with

- ➤ Fasting

- ➤ Weeping

- ➤ Mourning

Joel 2: 13 says:

"... Rend your heart and not your garments ..."

It was a common practice in times of grief to rend/tear your clothes in mourning. God wants a broken and torn spirit.

Now sin and judgement had touched every person – from the elders to the nursing babes. Repentance was to include every person. It was even to interrupt the bride and the bridegroom!

For as Joel 2: 17 says,

"Why should they say among the people, 'where is their God.'"

When you see these things begin to happen in a nation, then you need a leader to seek God in prayer and fasting and apply Biblical Principles.

Chapter 33

THE BENEFITS OF TRUSTING GOD

Many people do not see the importance and the significance of trusting God. Some don't believe in God, hence they don't trust what they don't believe in. Nevertheless, there are benefits for trusting God. Here are several of them.

➢ The key to prosperity is trust in God as your source at all times, and realizing that man is not your source.

➢ God is the One you must trust first; even if God placed a financial deliverer in your life God must always be at the forefront, not the deliverer.

➢ You must trust God first as your Chief Negotiator in business. While you may have good negotiation skills, God is the One you must trust to lead negotiations.

➢ You must trust God to deal with every aspect of our lives

➢ Trust God to promote you in due season

➢ Trust God to work out solutions when facing difficult situations.

➢ Trusting God first brings great prosperity in your lives.

➢ Your breakthrough is from the Lord first!

➢ Your help comes from the Lord (Psalm 121)

➢ Never shift focus when your blessing starts! Always trust God first according to Matthew 6: 33

➢ When someone makes a vow to you, always trust God to pay that vow. Don't put all your trust in the person to pay that vow. Instead, put all your trust in God to pay that vow. Otherwise, that vow will never be paid.

➢ Don't trust in your wealth and riches, trust in God.

➢ Don't trust in *'chariots and horses'* trust in God. Your security lies in God not in the things He allows you to have. You can only trust God to secure you and your assets, companies and nations.

➢ Trust in the Lord with all your heart and lean not to your own understanding. This is His request according to Proverbs 3: 5 – 6 and Proverbs 3: 20 – 22.

➢ Do not trust in a political administration to bring change; trust God! Trust Him to bring the change; He will raise up someone with His heart – one who trusts in Him, to make the necessary change.

➤ Do not trust the financial sector nor market conditions to determine whether or not your investment will be secured. Instead, trust in the Lord that even if the market is not booming, your investment is still booming.

➤ Do not put your trust in a man to correct a bad financial market. Instead, put your trust in God to fix a bad economy. (Jeremiah 9: 23 -24)

Read also Jeremiah 17 and I Timothy 4: 10

BIBLIOGRAPHY

Hagee, John C. General Editor, *Prophecy Study Bible*, (New King James Version) © 1997 Thomas Nelson, Inc

Hayford, Jack W. Executive Editor, *New Spirit-Filled Life®️ Bible,* (New King James Version) © 2002 Thomas Nelson, Inc.

Milligan, Ira L. *Understanding The Dreams You Dream,* First Edition. © 1997 Ira Milligan, Treasure House, An Imprint Of Destiny Image Inc.

Milligan, Ira L. *Understanding The Dreams You Dream Volume II,* Revised Edition. © 2000 Ira Milligan, Treasure House An Imprint Of Destiny Image Inc.

Pfeiffer, Charles F., Vos, Howard F., Rea, John. Editors, *Wycliffe Bible Dictionary*, (Seventh Printing) © 2005 Hendrickson Publishers, Inc

Price, Paula A. (PhD). *The Prophet's Dictionary: The Ultimate Guide To Supernatural Wisdom,* © 1999, 2002, 2006 Whittaker House

Strong, James. *The New Strong's Expanded Exhaustive Concordance of the Bible,* (Red Letter Edition) © 1990 Thomas Nelson Publishers

Concise Oxford English Dictionary Eleventh Edition. © 1964, 1976, 1982, 1990, 1995, 199, 2001, 2004 Oxford University Press. All Rights Reserved.

Made in the USA
Middletown, DE
26 November 2019